GREECE AND THE PERSIANS

Classical World series
(*Series Editor: Michael Gunningham*)

Classical World series

GREECE AND THE PERSIANS

John Sharwood Smith

Bristol Classical Press

General Editor: John H. Betts

First published in 1990 by
Bristol Classical Press, 226 North Street, Bedminster, Bristol BS3 1JD

© John Sharwood Smith, 1990

ISBN 1-85399-113-9

A CIP catalogue record for this book is available from the British Library

Printed in the United Kingdom by Billings & Sons Ltd.

TO F., WITH LOVE, FOR HER PATIENCE

Contents

Acknowledgements

This book owes a big debt to Amelie T.L. Kuhrt for criticisms and suggestions and for alerting me to the great precariousness and partiality of the evidence. Persisting errors are of course my own. I am indebted also to the encouragement and patience, and vigilance over matters of detail, of the Series Editor Michael Gunningham, and to Mrs C. Pendry for the use of photographs on pp. 7, 11 and 13.

List of Illustrations

Introduction

First encounters

As little as fifty years ago the encounter of the Greeks and Persians could have been described – without too much fear of contradiction – as a meeting of long lost cousins. For about two centuries it has been realised that all the languages known as Indo-European must have originated from a common source. This source was a language which was never written, and has therefore been irretrievably lost, but which can be partly reconstructed by ingenious linguistic detective work. The reconstructed language has been named 'Proto-Indo-European', and it represents, as far as is possible with present scholarly knowledge and techniques, the ancestor of most of the languages spoken today in Europe, Iran, Afghanistan, north India, and in parts of Central Asia. The same sort of detective work enabled scholars to guess certain things about the lives led by these speakers of 'Proto-Indo-European'. It appears that they knew how to work copper, practised some sort of agriculture, had domesticated cows and sheep, and worshipped a sky god – a father-figure who ruled in heaven just as, on earth, fathers ruled their sons, grandsons, and dependent womenfolk in their own tribal society.

Fifty years ago still further detective work seemed to have established that these first Indo-Europeans had lived in the grasslands of southern Russia and from there made their way in a series of migrations either westwards into Europe or eastwards into the lands on both sides of the Caspian Sea. A later migration took some of them into north-west India and others – the ancestors of the Persians – to north-east and finally south-west, Iran. Those who had gone westwards and southwards to the Mediterranean found the civilisation of Crete, while the ancestors of the Persians found themselves on the fringes of the very ancient civilisations of Mesopotamia. They also found, in control of these civilisations, speakers of Semitic languages – the family of languages which includes Arabic, Hebrew and Aramaic. These Semitic-speaking peoples had, like the Persians, been nomads before coming northwards from the grasslands that border

1

the Arabian Desert.

Ancient history then – according to accounts given in some of the textbooks written fifty years ago – consisted in the East, of the defeat by the Indo-European Iranians (Medes and Persians) of Semitic-speaking Assyrians and Babylonians and, in the West, the defeat of the Semitic-speaking naval powers of the Mediterranean (Phoenicians and Carthaginians) by, first, the Greeks and, afterwards, the Romans (both speakers of Indo-European languages). At the same time, since the Indo-European nations also fought among themselves, imperial rule moved steadily westwards, from Persians to Greeks and from Greeks to Romans.

In this neatly symmetrical pattern of ancient history, tall fair-haired Nordic peoples, having been the first to domesticate the horse, came as conquerors out of the steppes of Russia to confront slightly-built dark-haired Semitic peoples who had been the first to domesticate the ass and the camel and had come as conquerors out of the grasslands bordering the Arabian and Saharan deserts. This now seems *too* neat and *too* symmetrical. For one thing, scholars are no longer so confident about locating the original speakers of Proto-Indo-European in the steppes of Russia. (A new theory suggests that the languages may have originated in Anatolia with the people who first invented agriculture.) Another objection is that the horse (and chariot warfare) had been introduced into Mesopotamia long before the Iranian languages arrived. Moreover, archaeological evidence suggests that the speakers of the Iranian languages did not arrive in large numbers as conquering horsemen but moved southwards slowly with their herds of cattle and their ox-drawn wagons, avoiding, or surmounting with difficulty, many obstacles of mountain and desert and swamp. Far from sweeping into Iran as conquerors, they appear to have infiltrated, at intervals and in small groups, the valleys of the Iranian plateau where they finally settled. An important objection to the neat symmetrical pattern is that it assumes language and race to be identical, which is not the case. It has become quite clear that communities adopt the languages of other peoples (and forget their own) for a multitude of political, cultural and commercial reasons and not necessarily as the result of conquest.

On the other hand it is undeniable that the empire of the Persian kings was conquered by Alexander, that his Macedonian successors ruled between them Egypt, the Levant, Asia Minor, and, for a time, Mesopotamia, Iran and Central Asia, and that the Romans in turn conquered what was left of these lands after the Iranian Parthians had conquered Mesopotamia and the lands east of it. Furthermore, there *is* a certain historical symmetry in the ebb and flow of conflict between East and West: between the Parthians of Iran and the Roman emperors; between the kings of a revived Persia (the so-called Sassanid dynasty) and the rulers of the Byzantine Empire; between the Muslim Arabs who overran Asia Minor, north Africa and Spain and the crusaders of the eleventh to the thirteenth centuries; and finally, after the capture of Constantinople, between the Ottoman Turks and the nations of eastern Europe. Although this is a story of aggressive hostility and repeated conflict, both East and West have nonetheless owed much to the traffic of ideas and technology that has passed between them in each direction. This has included the development by the Greeks, sometime before the eighth century BC, of an alphabet based on that of the Phoenicians; also the acquisition of Greek philosophy, science and medicine by the Arabs in the ninth century AD. From the East the Greeks learnt astronomy and mathematics (from Babylon), naval warfare (from the Phoenicians), free-standing sculpture (from Egypt or Syria). The Persian kings were also great borrowers in the interest of creating an imperial style of art and architecture. Forms and motifs were borrowed from Egypt and Mesopotamia as well as derived from previous civilisations nearer their homeland. From the Greeks they borrowed building techniques and they used Greek masons (among others) to build their palaces. They employed Greek doctors to look after their health (and that of their families) and Greek mercenary soldiers to help police their empire. As rulers of a large, rich and powerful empire they could attract from beyond their borders men with specialist skills and the desire for greater rewards than were available at home.

The major moments of crisis in the conflict between East and West have all been of significance to the history of Europe (and therefore, since European culture has spread world-wide, of significance to the world) but no crisis can have been more significant than the invasion of Greece by the Persian monarch Xerxes and its defeat. The justification for calling the battles of Marathon, Salamis and Plataea 'decisive' is the same as that for calling the Battle of Britain 'decisive'. In each case what hung in the balance was not merely a decision about territory, or the subjection of one people to another, but the triumph and failure of ideologies with vast implications for the future of mankind.

The focus of this book is Xerxes' attempt to include Greece in his empire. Before starting him on his great expedition it seems sensible to sketch in something of the background to his personal power, his immense dominions and the antecedents of the Persian Empire. And after describing his failure it seems worthwhile to contrast his expedition into Greece with the story of an adventure that took Greeks into the heart of the Persian Empire.

Chapter 1
The Palace and the King

> I am Khshayarsha the King, King of Kings, King of the lands, son of Darayavaush the King, of the family of Hakamanish, a Persian, son of a Persian. Thus says Khshayarsha the King. By the favour of Ahuramazda, these are the lands over which I am king...

This inscription was found in the ruins of an immense palace standing on a terrace built at the foot of a mountain and overlooking a plain. The plain is several thousand feet above sea level and 'bathed in a light of a purity unequalled anywhere else in the world' (in the view of a modern art scholar). The inscription is in cuneiform (wedge-shaped) letters carved with a chisel into the stonework.

The Bible as history

At the beginning of the nineteenth century empty stretches of the Middle East were littered with dusty mounds beneath which lay the ruins of ancient cities waiting – or so it must have seemed – to be uncovered by eager excavators. In the nineteenth century virtually everyone was familiar with the Bible, every chapter of which was supposed by most readers to be literally true. But there were sceptics; so popular, as well as scholarly, interest was aroused when it became known in Europe that there were learned enthusiasts ready to enlist armies of Arab workmen to dig up the ancient past. By digging up the palaces of Shalmanesar and Sennacherib, kings of Assyria, of Nebuchadnezzar and Belshazzar, kings of Babylon, and of Darius 'the Median' and his son 'Ahasuerus', it was hoped that the excavators might prove, even to the sceptics, that the Bible was historically true.

Everyone had read in the Second Book of Kings, Chapter 17, that Shalmanesar had captured Samaria and carried off the Israelites. In Chapter 19 it was told that Sennacherib retreated from Jerusalem when the angel of the Lord smote 'an hundred four-score and five thousand' of his soldiers. Chapter 24 related that Nebuchadnezzar came to Jerusalem and carried off 'all the mighty men of valour...and

5

Fig. 1. The ruins of Persepolis from the air.

all the craftsmen and smiths'. The Book of Esther told the story of how Ahasuerus, who 'reigned from India even unto Ethiopia' spared the Jews in his kingdom for the sake of Esther. Finally Belshazzar, according to Chapter 5 of the Book of Daniel, 'made a great feast' and saw the writing on the wall and was slain by 'Darius the Median', who took his kingdom.

Not only all this, but perhaps, it was hoped by some, the excavators might even find traces of the Garden of Eden and relics of our first parents.

Excavators and decipherers

The ruins of the Palace of Khshayarsha ('Ahasuerus' to the writer of the Book of Esther) did not suffer quite as drastically from the decay

Fig. 2. The ruins of Persepolis.

and neglect that befell ancient palaces and cities once they ceased to be important. It was not built over like Priam's Troy, nor quarried for the building of nearby towns and villages as happened to Babylon. Though most of the palace was buried by the sands of time, enough of it remained uncovered to attract the curiosity of European travellers from as early as the seventeenth century.

From the first, scholars were intrigued by the cuneiform inscriptions, copies of which were brought back to Europe to be pored over in France, Germany, Denmark, Ireland and England. Soon it was realised that the inscriptions were in three languages and that one of these – Old Persian – was close to Sanskrit (the language of the religious scriptures of India). This made the decipherment of the Persian texts not too difficult for scholars who had learnt Sanskrit from the Brahmins of India. However the first breakthrough was made by an obscure German schoolmaster who knew no oriental languages at all, but worked by the methods of cryptography.

The task was completed by an English soldier, scholar and diplomat, Sir Henry Rawlinson, who tackled the most extensive and inaccessible of all the inscriptions of the Persian kings – the long recital, in three languages, of his achievements which Khshayarsha's father Darayavaush had caused to be inscribed, together with a picture of himself, 500 feet up a sheer rock overlooking a much used caravan-route from Iran to Babylonia. With quite amazing nerve and agility, and the help of a 'wild Kurdish boy', Rawlinson copied, in 1844, the entire text.

The three languages proved to be: Old Persian, Akkadian (the language of Babylonia) and the language of the ancient kingdom of Elam (which lay between Babylonia and the Zagros mountains).

Who, then, were Khshayarsha and Darayavaush? They are known to Europeans as Xerxes and Darius because that is what the Greeks called them (to be precise the Greeks called Darayavaush 'Dareios' but the Romans Latinised this to 'Darius', and that is how the name was transmitted in European literature (including the English Bible). Khshayarsha was 'Xerxes' to both Greeks and Romans.

Historians of Persia

Before the excavation of the palace revealed not only the inscriptions but also clay tablets containing palace records, the deeds and life-style of Darius and Xerxes and of the other eleven Persian Great Kings, were known almost exclusively from what had been written about them by Greeks. This creates a serious problem for modern historians who still have very little with which to counterbalance the self-flattering distortions and plain misunderstandings transmitted by Greek writers. In the last few decades, however, some progress has been made.

Herodotus of Halicarnassus was born a subject of Xerxes and travelled about the western lands of the Persian Empire asking all sorts of questions – through interpreters where necessary since he spoke, it appears, no language except Greek – in order to write about the manners and customs of the Persians and other peoples of the Empire. This was to be part of his great story of how the Greeks and Persians became enemies and how Xerxes brought his vast army to Greece and was defeated.

Three other Greeks wrote interestingly about Persia and the Persians from personal knowledge. One of these, Xenophon, described what happened when, eighty years after Xerxes' invasion, he joined the army of a Persian prince who set out from the westernmost provinces of Persia to the heart of the Empire to kill his brother and take his place as Great King. The other two Greeks who wrote about Persia from personal knowledge were successively doctors to the Persian royal family: Ktesias and Dinon.

Xenophon's writings have survived. For a number of reasons none of them are thought to be wholly reliable, least of all the fanciful biography he wrote of Cyrus the Great, the founder of the Persian Empire. This is not so much a biography as a treatise on how to be a good and great king, and is full of obvious fictions. The writings of Ktesias and Dinon have been lost, but were used or quoted by later Greek writers in works that have survived. Living, as they did, at the Persian court for a good number of years they must have been well-informed about court matters – conspiracies and punishments, intrigues and revenges. Ktesias' account of Xerxes' invasion of Greece seems to have often contradicted Herodotus. Herodotus was a child at the time of Xerxes' invasion and so able, when he grew up, to talk to people – generals and political leaders as well as ordinary people – who were involved in the wars on one side or the other. Ktesias, on the other hand, lived at least a generation later than Herodotus and does not seem to have had access to Persian sources of any value, so scholars do not take much notice of his attempts to discredit Herodotus. Herodotus may well have been misled from time to time by the Persians he talked to about the early history of Persia, but, as regards the course of Xerxes' invasion, he seems to have used fairly accurate information – until he comes to assess the size of the Persian armament. But then fighting men have always tended to exaggerate the numbers and casualties of their enemies.

Another ancient Greek historian who wrote about Persia was Diodorus the Sicilian who, about five hundred years after the time of Xerxes, compiled from previous writers an immense history of the world (as he envisaged it). Two thirds of it have perished, which is not a great loss as he was incapable of distinguishing myth from history. For this reason he is despised by modern scholars, but he is also appreciated by them, since he gives them occasion to exercise their skill in detecting which previous author he is copying in any particular chapter of his work. Sometimes his source may be a reputable author whose work is lost, and in these cases he may incorporate information not otherwise available. He was the source for Shelley's famous poem 'Ozymandias'. In Chapter 4 of the first book of his universal history he describes, at second or third hand, the tomb of Pharoah Ramses II ('Ozymandias') of Egypt and its boastful inscription. He, however, believed the statue to be a very fine one. The 'frown and wrinkled lip, and sneer of cold command' were invented by Shelley as appropriate for an ancient (or modern) tyrant.

Xerxes' inscription, with comments

(a) The succession
'I am Xerxes the King,' he says. He became king in the year 486 BC, succeeding his father Darius. Darius had sent an expedition to Greece under one of his generals and it had met with a sharp defeat. In the three years before he died he was busy organising the forces of his Empire for a second expedition, which he probably intended to lead himself. Just before his death the province of Egypt, conquered forty years before, revolted and had to be reconquered. Then there were two revolts in Babylonia which had to be suppressed. In 481 Xerxes was ready to set out with his huge army for Greece.

(b) Title
'King of Kings,' he says. This title was regularly used by the Persian kings with some justification. Xerxes' empire had absorbed the kingdoms of Media, Lydia, Assyria, Elam and other minor states and cities of Mesopotamia and Egypt, as well as the petty kingdoms of the

Levant which featured importantly in the history of Palestine and the Jews.

(c) Provinces
'King of the Lands.' There were twenty provinces in the Persian Empire which stretched from Afghanistan to the Mediterranean Sea, from the Black Sea and the Caucasus Mountains to the Sahara, and from the deserts beyond the Oxus River to the Indian Ocean.

Fig. 3. Persian Scenery.

(d) Paternity

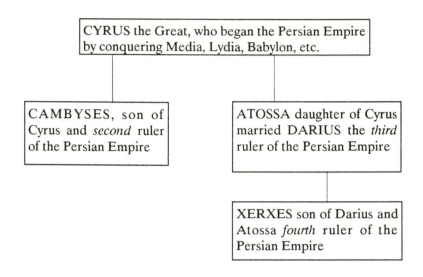

Xerxes' family tree

'Son of Darius the King.' Darius, Xerxes' father, was not born to be king, being at most a very distant cousin (and possibly no relation at all) of Cyrus the Great, the founder of the Persian Empire. Cyrus' son Cambyses had added Egypt to the Empire and then died mysteriously on his way back to Persia, where an equally mysterious conspiracy had set a pretender on the throne – or so we are led to believe by the inscription on the rock of Behistun – the one which Sir Henry Rawlinson risked his life to copy. In this inscription Xerxes' father Darius claims that wicked conspirators, prompted by 'The Lie' (by which he meant the spirit opposed to Ahura-Mazda, the God of Truth and Justice), deceived the Median and Persian nobility into believing that a certain Median priest – one of the Magi – was Cambyses' brother and therefore his legitimate successor, whereas Cambyses had, in fact, had this brother secretly murdered. The Behistun inscription narrates that Darius led six noble Persians to assassinate the impostor and so, by the favour of Ahura-Mazda, became Great King himself. (But he had to put down rebellions in many parts of the Empire to make good his claim to the title.)

Fig. 4. Procession of Persian noblemen bearing gifts: depicted on Persepolis relief.

Seeing that Darius' Behistun inscription is propaganda (translated copies were sent to the principal cities of the Empire) it is not likely to be wholly truthful. Indeed scholars are inclined to believe that the 'impostor' may have been a true son of Cyrus the Great who had offended the Persian nobility by ceasing to reward them with a status superior to that of the other subjects of the Empire.

(e) Ancestry
'of the family of Hakamanish,' continues Xerxes' inscription. Hakamanish (the Greeks wrote his name Akhaimenes, the Romans and ourselves Achaemenes) was the ancestor of Cyrus the Great –

Fig. 5. Darius triumphs over his enemies: the Behistun relief and inscriptions

great great grandfather, if the inscriptions tell the truth – and was claimed (perhaps falsely) as an ancestor by Darius; so the Great Kings of Persia after Darius called themselves Achaemenians (or Achaemenids) and are so referred to by scholars today.

(f) Xerxes' religion

Xerxes says that he ruled the Persian Empire 'by the favour of Ahura-Mazda'. Just as the Medes and the Persians spoke a language which shared a common ancestor with the language spoken in north India, so the religion of the Medes and Persians developed from a religion which gave many of its gods to the Hindu religion of India. The Persian religion, however, at some time before the days of Cyrus the Great, was reformed by a great religious teacher called Zoroaster. There are no contemporary accounts of Zoroaster's life and it is not certain when or where he lived or what precisely he taught, or whether the religious beliefs implied by Achaemenian inscriptions were Zoroastrian.

These beliefs imply a God, Ahura-Mazda, who upholds Justice and Truth, and is supported by the *ahuras*, the good spirits of the universe, against the *daivas*, evil spirits of darkness and lies.

In addition to Ahura-Mazda the Persian kings recognised the gods worshipped by the various peoples of the Empire. To each shrine and its priests they were prepared to give assistance in acknowledgement of the goodwill they considered they had received from that particular god. But if the worshippers of that god revolted then the god was considered hostile and his shrines suffered accordingly.

Darius, in his Behistun inscription, says that in killing the impostor he was helped by Ahura-Mazda and 'the other gods who are', and the reasons he gives for receiving their help are:

> because I was not wicked, nor a liar, nor cruel, neither I nor my family. I thought always of right and justice. Neither to noblemen nor to poor people have I done violence.

The relief carvings

The Persian Great Kings liked to indicate to their subjects that they were under the protection of Ahura-Mazda. This they did by having his symbol carved as if he were hovering in the sky near to them. He can be seen in the picture on p. 14. Darius is carved rather larger than anyone else on the frieze and is shown with his right hand raised, perhaps in thanks to Ahura-Mazda for having helped him to conquer the kings and nobles who refused to recognise him as Great King at the beginning of his reign. He has had these kings and nobles carved as if roped together before him, while he stands with his foot on the prostrate body of the 'impostor', who raises his arms to plead for mercy – which neither he nor the others got. Mutilation and exposure to public mockery before death was the fate reserved for dangerous enemies and that was the fate of at least two of those shown on this relief; the others were merely put to death. The relief is not to be taken literally, as the kings were captured and executed in separate campaigns and in different parts of the Empire, while the 'impostor' was surprised and assassinated in his fortress palace in Media.

This carved picture must have been the most effective part of Darius' propaganda message on the Behistun rock. The inscriptions can hardly have been readable by anyone journeying past, five hundred feet below, even if many of Darius' subjects had known how to read (Darius himself and his nobles almost certainly did not: they would have had secretaries to do their reading for them). The very impressive picture, however, would serve to remind travellers of the *message* of the inscriptions. This would be familiar to most subjects of the Empire, including the illiterate. Even though they could not read either the Behistun inscriptions or the translations displayed in their region, yet they would have known from others just what their story and their message was.

Both the Behistun inscriptions and the picture would have been, it is reasonable to believe, of personal importance to Darius. Other kings who had ruled in Mesopotamia had left memorials of their greatness to impress later generations, and Darius would arguably want to do so also. The story of his great deeds would be forever there carved in the Elamite language and in the Akkadian language. Then he invented a script for writing the Persian language – never before written – and added a revised inscription in that. The engravers who carved the incriptions had worked from a ledge of rock on which they could stand in some sort of comfort and security. Darius had this ledge cut away so that no later king could send other engravers up to tamper with his message, or erase it: so there it remained for about two and a half thousand years before Sir Henry Rawlinson came to decipher it. And there it still remains.

Chapter 2
Similarities and Contrasts

Physical environments

Although the Greek and Persian languages are traceable to a common origin it is no longer supposed, as by some people it once was, that all those who spoke Greek or Persian in the fifth century BC belonged to a specially dominant, or specially creative, Indo-European (also known as 'Aryan') race. Scholars are more likely to point to the influence of physical environment in determining the destiny of a people than to any real or imaginary racial characteristics. This is especially true of the ancient world where terrain and climate dictated the conditions of life, since there was little in the way of technology to improve on what nature provided. The highly organised monarchies of the great river valleys did have a partial substitute for technology in their ability to direct the mass labour required to construct and maintain elaborate irrigation works, but even on these monarchies nature imposed an iron rule: they must control the flood waters or perish.

In the physical environment of the Greeks and Persians there were similarities and significant differences.

The corner of the Iranian plateau where the Persians finally settled was a harsh land in which only those flourished who were tough in mind and body. It was a land of three contrasting zones. There was a hot, dry and barren area on the coast; an upland area of grassy valleys which provided good grazing for sheep, cattle and horses, was well-watered, in parts well-wooded and suitable for fruit growing. Furthest inland there was an inhospitable area of rocks, high mountains and snow. Contrasts between the seasons were everywhere stark: bitterly cold winters followed by torrid summers.

The geography of the Greek peninsula is much more complex because of the contrary influences of the mountains and the sea. The mountain ranges which run the length of the peninsula from north to south are heavily forested, snow-covered in winter and sparsely populated by hardy highlanders who live in small villages. The mountain uplands provide pasture for cattle, pigs and goats and for

17

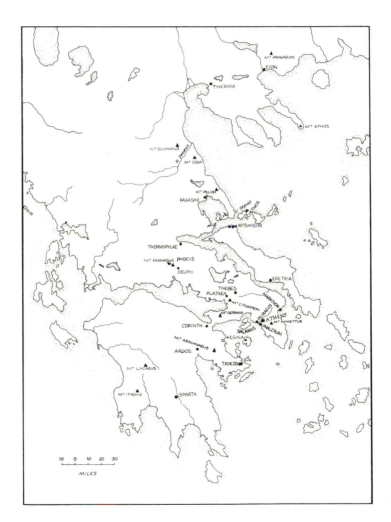

Fig. 6. Mainland Greece.

sheep which are brought down each autumn to winter in the lowlands. The spurs of the mountain ranges embrace small areas of lowland plain and cut these off from one another so effectively that communication in ancient times was difficult in summer and often impossible in winter. Each of these plains has its own particular terrain and climate. Where they border on the sea their seasonal changes of temperature are far less extreme than they are in the Iranian valleys; but where they are land-locked, the winters are bitter enough. Some of the plains are fertile and will produce cereal crops, some even have pasture for horse-rearing and cattle-breeding, but more often they have thin soil suitable only for the vine and the olive.

This diversity of the lowland enclaves and their isolation from one another made it difficult for the Greeks who had settled in them to live together in large groups under tribal leaders as the Medes and Persians did. Instead, whenever they and their flocks were threatened by pirates or other maurauders from the sea, they gathered on some easily defensible outcrop of rock a little way inland, while continuing, when the danger had passed, to live in small villages to farm the land.

In time the rock of refuge became a focus for all the inhabitants of the area: the chief market; the residence of the tribal chief or king; and a political centre for debate and decision. Some of the farmers came and lived at the foot of the rock, and there gathered the craftsmen and traders. In this way there arose small self-contained city-states (*poleis*, sing. *polis*), always ready to quarrel with other city-states the other side of the mountains or across the sea. This made them very different from the Persians, who remained a mainly pastoral people, loosely organised in tribes.

Geography made the sea an ever present element in the lives of the Greeks. Travel and transport from any one part of Greece to any other, difficult by land because of the trackless mountains, was, except in the stormy winter months, easy by sea. Each new group of pastoralists who arrived in Greece, driving their flocks with them and mingling with, or driving out or subjugating the people already there, found the sea a strange and frightening element. In the course of time those who settled on lands by the sea coast became familiar with this new element and, like all their predecessors, learnt to be adventurous seamen, explorers, traders, pirates and founders of overseas colonies.

The Persians, on the other hand, had no great need of sea communications. Roads, however, became essential when they acquired their empire. They took over from the Assyrians the idea of a royal mail service and perfected it. Their most celebrated route (described by Herodotus) ran from Sardis to Susa. It was about 1,600 miles long, had 111 staging posts and a number of guard houses. Along this road travelled the royal messengers.

> There is nothing mortal that is swifter than these men...It is said that the route is furnished with horses and men for each day's journey. Neither snow nor rain, neither the heat of day nor the darkness of night will prevent them from completing their appointed journey in the quickest possible time. The first despatch rider hands his despatch to the second and the second to the third – and so on, just like the torch relay-race held by the Greeks in honour of Hephaistos.
>
> (HERODOTUS, 8.98)

When the Persians' conquests had brought them to the eastern Mediterranean coastline from Egypt to the Hellespont they were quick to make use of the naval power they derived from the fleets of their subjects – Egyptians, Phoenicians and Ionian Greeks in particular. In Xerxes' expedition the subject peoples seem to have provided the rowers and the captains, the Persians the admirals and the marines.

By contrast with the mainland Greeks the Persians had every facility for breeding horses and training cavalry. According to Herodotus, who claims to speak from personal knowledge, every Persian boy was taught three things only: to ride, to shoot with the bow and to tell the truth. Not surprisingly the Persians were formidable in archery and had an elite cavalry corps that completely outclassed anything the Greeks could put into the field.

Political experience and folk memories

It is obvious that peoples and cities are as they are not only because of their physical environment, but also because of what has happened to them in the past. In the ancient cities of Mesopotamia and Egypt, from a very early time, priests and royal scribes recorded events which they considered important. Neither the early Greeks nor the early Persians had either priests or royal scribes who kept records. This did not mean that their past was lost to them. Events were transformed into legends and passed on in story-telling and song. The legends of the Greeks found their way into poetry and drama and prose tales which were written down after the Greeks had become literate. In this way we have a very good idea of what they believed about their past. From the Persians we have only religious scriptures which tell of their beliefs about the gods and the origins of human beings and animals, but nothing about their history before Cyrus the Great. This has to be pieced together from references in the records of the Babylonians and Assyrians or from deductions made from the evidence of pottery and metal ornaments found and examined by archaeologists.

Political experience: the Persians

Until the Persians came out of their mountain valleys their political experience had been, as far as it can be deduced, straightforward and limited. They had arrived in their homeland under the leadership of their tribal chiefs and the heads of their clans. These, when they settled down in their new home, became their kings and their nobles. The tribes, though related, no doubt raided one another's flocks and from time to time fought against one another, as pastoral tribes have always done unless kept in order by some strong central power. Beyond the foothills of their homeland, north of the Persian Gulf, was the ancient kingdom of Elam. For two thousand years, under a succession of dynasties, Elam had been an important kingdom with wide trading connections. In its two thousand years of existence the Elamites had experienced many political and military reversals, conquering nearby monarchies, killing their kings and carrying off their gods, then in turn suffering the same fate themselves. For a long time the kingdom of Elam included the mountainous lands that the Persians came to occupy, and there its kings had their capital, in a city named Anshan. When this area was lost the capital was transferred to Elam's second city, Susa.

By the seventh century BC, while the kings of Elam were occupied with the task of holding off the aggressive, ever victorious, armies of Assyria, Anshan had become a Persian capital, ruled by the grandfather of Cyrus the Great. In the middle of the seventh century the King of Elam rashly challenged Assyria's terrible King Assurbanipal. He was defeated and beheaded in front of his own army, and Susa was sacked. Elam suffered further invasions by Assurbanipal and at this time the Assyrian tablets record that a Cyrus sent his son as hostage to Assurbanipal, together with many presents. This Cyrus may be the grandfather of Cyrus the Great, successfully persuading Assurbanipal not to attack and sack Anshan.

There are indications that the kingdom of Elam, with its

sophisticated culture and written language, influenced the more backward Persians. There must have been trade between them, as the sheep-farming and cattle-farming of the Persians would have complemented the entirely different economy of the Elamites, who had a hot lowland climate and complex irrigation systems. There are records, too, of attempts by the rulers of Elam to involve the Persian chieftains in their wars against Assyria.

Persians and Medes

It had been fortunate for the Persians that Elam stood between them and the Assyrian Empire. This had enabled them to escape the destructive power of the Assyrian war machine. Their Iranian cousins, the Medes, were not so lucky. The lands they occupied were close to the eastern boundaries of the Assyrian Empire. For 200 years they suffered periodic invasions to demand tribute or to punish them for not paying it, or for assisting Assyria's enemies. The effect of these invasions was to make the Medes come together with neighbouring communities and organise themselves under a single ruler.

Herodotus' account of how the Median kingdom arose is precise and picturesque, but scholars now think it was based on legend rather than reality. However it is clear that unification under single kings did take place, and that a king named Cyaxares, at the end of the seventh century BC, was strong enough to join with the ruler of Babylon in attacking Assyria. Together they captured, one by one, all the cities of the Assyrians and destroyed Assyria as a military power.

The Persians take over

Cyrus the Great began his rule as King of Anshan. As with most great men, legends were told of his birth and childhood. Herodotus retold one of them and wrote that he knew three others. Ktesias also recounted a legend that has been preserved. It is quite different from that of Herodotus. Both have every resemblance to folktales, but Herodotus gives a detail that may be true (but is not supported by other evidence): that Cyrus' mother was the daughter of Astyages, the son of Cyaraxares, King of the Medes. Herodotus also says that as a Persian he was a subject of Astyages, but from the Babylonian evidence it seems that this is not true.

There is, scholars tell us, cuneiform evidence to suggest that for the first nine years of his reign Cyrus was busy asserting his authority over his own little kingdom. Then he clashed with Astyages. Astyages collected an army to conquer Cyrus' kingdom, but, according to a Babylonian chronicle, the army rebelled, took him prisoner and handed him over to Cyrus.

As ruler of both the Persians and Medes Cyrus was no longer an unimportant kinglet ruling over a number of hardy, unsophisticated, pastoral tribes. He had become, instead, the ruler of an extensive empire. He was one of the great conquerors of history, but he was not *merely* a conqueror: he also knew how to make his rule acceptable to most ot the peoples he had conquered. How he achieved this is illustrated by three actions he took when he captured Babylon. He restored the temple of the great Babylonian god Marduk and sent back to their own cities the images of the gods which Nabunaid, the last ruler of Babylon, had taken away to Babylon. Secondly, he took an interest in those Jews who had been taken captive to Babylon by Nebuchadnezzar, and encouraged them to return to Jerusalem to rebuild their temple. Thirdly, he installed himself in the magnificent Royal Palace of Babylon, as if he were not so much a conqueror as the founder of a new Babylonian dynasty.

In the thirtieth year of his reign he was killed while fighting a Scythian tribe in the desert regions at the extreme north-east frontier of his empire.

The simple hardy tribal leaders of a pastoral people had become, in consequence of Cyrus' conquests, the aristocracy of a vast empire of immense wealth, containing cities like Susa, Babylon, Sardis in Lydia, Damascus in Syria, Jerusalem, Tyre and Sidon in Palestine, all of which had for centuries been highly civilised.

Political experience: the Greeks

The Greek civilisation of the fifth century BC was not entirely new. Before it there had been a Dark Age, but before that there had been in Greece an elaborate civilisation of great palaces and wide-ruling kings who had fought and traded and formed alliances with the cities and kingdoms of Asia Minor. Memories of this great age of Mycenaean civilisation formed the basis of Greek legends and traditions, and the ruins of the great palaces could still be seen in the fifth century.

The Dark Age had been a time of devastation, conquest and flight. Civilisation had returned in the shape of city-states slowly forming in the many enclaves between the mountains. Emerging first as petty kingdoms they changed in the course of time to aristocracies, to tyrannies, to democracies or to various combinations of these three forms of government.

At the beginning of the fifth century the two most powerful city-states were Sparta and Athens.

Sparta was not, strictly speaking, a city-state at all, as there was no city, only open villages. The Spartans had subjugated the inhabitants of the neighbouring countryside and obliged them to work the land for them. Being greatly outnumbered the Spartans were only able to do this by devoting their lives to becoming, and remaining, the world's best soldiers. They had no time for commerce and very little time for any sort of cultural activities. They sternly resisted any change to their way of life, kept their two kings (from quite separate families) but allowed them limited power (though one or other of them always commanded the army). Only reluctantly did they ever undertake any campaign away from their own part of Greece.

Athens was a great commercial centre and had recently suffered a period of class-war. Thanks to reforms introduced by two far-sighted statesmen the quarrels between the classes had been settled and the Athenians had begun their progress towards out-and-out democracy.

By contrast with the conservative Spartans, the Athenians were enterprising to the point of rashness, imaginative and artistically creative as no other state (with the possible exception of Florence in the early Renaissance) has ever been. Sparta, because of her invincible army, was acknowledged by other city-states as their natural leader in any crisis that might affect all the states of Greece; but, if we are to believe Herodotus (who was patently biased in favour of Athens), it was the Athenian Themistocles who planned the strategy adopted by the Greeks to counter the first impact of the Persian invasion.

Chapter 3
More Contrasts and First Clashes

Contrasting life-styles: the Persians

The lives of the Persian nobility were transformed by the conquests of Cyrus the Great. Enormous wealth was acquired for Cyrus' treasury from the conquered kings of Babylon and Lydia, and tribute flowed in from all the peoples of the Empire. The nobles, from tribal chieftains, became governors of provinces and were rewarded with estates and other gifts which enabled them to live as kings in their own palaces, to eat off gold plates and drink from jewelled goblets, to lay out parks and gardens, to keep beautiful women in their harems and fine horses in their stables, and with these to hunt all the wild animals to be found within the Empire, from ostriches to lions.

Although they lived like kings, and had the power of kings in the provinces they governed, the nobles were still the humble servitors of the Great King (Greek writers sometimes used the word *doulos* [slave] of the relationship). The Great Kings's wealth and magnificence was always a hundred times greater than that of his nobles and *his* power was limitless. In the picture on p. 26 we see him sitting on his throne, sceptre in hand, prepared to receive one of his subjects in audience. His throne is lofty so he needs a stool for his feet. Before him are two incense-burners to perfume the air, and facing him is the chief palace official who carries his staff of office, and holds his other hand before his mouth in a gesture of respect (lesser officials would have had to prostrate themselves). The king is more than life-size, as is the Crown Prince who stands behind him. Both king and prince wear expressions of wisdom and benevolence, unlike the statue in Shelley's poem 'Ozymandias', with its frown and sneer. Shelley seems to have imagined that the sculptor was free to portray his Pharaoh as he saw him, whereas with ancient royalty (as, by and large, with modern) an artist would be constrained by the artistic conventions of the time e.g. the treatment of the hair and beards in the picture on p. 26) and by the necessity of portraying the royal personage as he wished to be seen by his subjects and by later generations.

Fig. 7. Darius giving audience: depicted on Persepolis' relief.

Palace life-style

It might well be thought that to be a Great King of Persia was an enviable destiny. Unlimited power over all the inhabitants, regardless of rank, of twenty provinces; three spectacular palaces, each appropriate for a different time of the year, as well as one in Babylon and others in more distant parts of the Empire; a harem of 360 women recruited from the length and breadth of the Empire; inexhaustible wealth in gold and precious stones, and treasures of craftsmanship of which the griffins on the bracelet illustrated on p. 27 are an example. On the other hand the Great King had to observe rigid patterns of behaviour laid down in court etiquette. He had to eat screened from his nobles by a curtain. He must not go on foot outside his palace, and wherever he went he was surrounded by menials carrying napkins, parasols, flywhisks, scent bottles and censers. He wore, over a striped tunic and crimson trousers, a long purple robe, with full sleeves, embroidered in gold. Certain nobles were always in attendance – his bow-and-quiver bearer, his battle-axe bearer and the commander of his palace guard.

Cyrus, Cambyses and Darius were great warriors and spent much of their time on campaign. So did Xerxes at the beginning of his reign. Later kings led their armies against revolted provinces and troublesome highlanders, but from Xerxes' successor onwards they appear in Greek literature less in connection with their military activities than with sexual scandals, family feuds, conspiracies and assassinations. There is little in the way of other sources to contradict this picture of monarchs corrupted by a self-indulgent life-style and manipulated by their women – a picture which (since the Empire continued to function efficiently) must be, to say the least, overdrawn.

Fig. 8. Griffin bracelet: part of a gold and silver treasure found in the River Oxus, dating from Achaemenid times.

Esther

In uncovering the buried cities the excavators raised more questions about the historical truth of the Bible than they answered. The Book of Esther now seems to be not history but a fable, written some 400 years after the lifetime of Xerxes, at whose court the story is set. It does, however, reflect the impression made throughout the Middle East by the splendour and the power of the kings of Persia.

> The king made a feast unto all the people who were present in Shushan the Palace [the city of Susa] both unto great and small, seven days, in the court of the garden of the king's palace; where there were white green and blue hangings fastened with cords of fine linen and purple to silver rings

and pillars of marble; the beds were of gold and silver, upon a pavement of red, and blue and white, and black marble. And they gave them drink in vessels of gold (the vessels being diverse one from another), and royal wine in abundance, according to the state of the king.

(THE BOOK OF ESTHER, Chap. 1)

It seems unlikely that any king of Persia ever entertained all the inhabitants of Susa, but the palace records dug up at Persepolis show that he could easily have done so if he had wished.

Contrasting life-styles: the Greeks

There had been tyrants in Greece in the century before the expedition of Xerxes, and these had made some display of local magnificence, but their magnificence was trivial by comparison with the splendours of the Persian court.* By the fifth century the tyrants on the mainland of Greece had all been killed or driven out and personal extravagance had become unfashionable (and unwise, since it was dangerous for an aristocrat to give the impression that he might be aiming to become a tyrant). The tyrants' example, however, of lavish expense on temples and public buildings, and on organising religious festivals, was carried on by the governments that followed them whenever public funds were available.

Even in democratically-inclined Athens there were class distinctions. There were aristocrats who had inherited estates and were wealthy enough to have the leisure and the money for a social life of elegant banqueting and for hunting and athletics and competing in the Olympic Games – some of them even wealthy enough to train teams of horses for the chariot-racing events (the driving, however, was left to professional charioteers). They served in the cavalry when their *polis* went to war, supplying their own horses, or else they equipped, maintained and served in a warship. In the early fifth century they dominated politics even in democratic Athens.

Next in rank were those farmers who were prosperous enough to afford a suit of armour and serve in the front-line infantry – the hoplites. These were, militarily and politically, the backbone of the *polis*.

---

* For detailed information see *Athens under the Tyrants* by J.A. Smith, in this series.

Below them came the sailors, craftsmen and artisans who rowed in the navy, and the poor countrymen who served as light-armed troops.

At Athens the wealthy were required to spend, from time to time, much money in equipping and maintaining ships for the Athenian navy, in training and equipping actors for the drama festivals, in paying for the training of athletes and the staging of athletic contests and in equipping and supervising certain religious activities. All these expenses brought them honour and distinction, as did any victories they achieved with their chariots. The wealthy, brilliant, but unreliable statesman Alcibiades is said to have gained great prestige by entering seven chariots at the Olympic Games, winning first, second and fourth prizes. This was only one of his many extravagances, which tended to outrun his means. Yet the life-style of Greek aristocrats, even that of Alcibiades, would have seemed poverty-stricken to a Persian nobleman: no large town or country houses; no costly clothes or furniture; tableware elegant, perhaps, but not sumptuous; no ornamental gardens nor parks stocked with game; few domestic slaves; and no lavish profusion of food and drink at their banquets.

At Sparta (which was unique among city-states) there was no trade and no coinage, and all the farming was done by the serfs for the benefit of their masters the Spartiates – the full citizens of Sparta. These, from boyhood onwards, led the hard existence of soldiers in perpetual training, healthily fed, well exercised and hardened by an open air life with no luxuries.

We know little in detail about the daily life in other city-states. Corinth, which had profitable trade with Sicily and the western Mediterranean, was regarded as vulgarly rich, but only by Greek standards. Such were the economic circumstances of Greece that hard agricultural labour, poverty and, in bad years, near starvation must have been the general lot.

On the other hand at Athens and in other city-states (but not Sparta) life was culturally very rich. There were festivals and processions to watch or take part in, and everywhere beautiful public buildings embellished with beautiful sculptures or beautiful paintings. There was choral music to listen to and plays – both tragedies and comedies – to attend.

Early contacts between Greeks and Persians

(a) Ionia

In the Dark Ages of Greece many Greeks had fled from their homelands on the mainland to found new cities on the coast of Asia Minor. These Greeks were a mixed collection from many areas of Greece but, as they all set out across the Aegean Sea from Attica, so they always felt a certain kinship with the Athenians. They called themselves Ionians (as the Athenians did) and the coast of Asia Minor became known as Ionia. As civilisation on the mainland recovered from the devastation of the Dark Age, the population of the new city-states grew to be greater than the land could support; so new colonies were planned and colonists sent out to the Bosphorus and the Black Sea or to Italy and Sicily or further west still.

In the beginning of the seventh century the kingdom of Lydia (whose capital was at Sardis, not more than 70 miles from the Aegean coast) became powerful and prosperous under a new dynasty and began to threaten the Ionian cities of Asia Minor. Towards the middle of the sixth century, the fifth king of the new dynasty, Croesus, was powerful enough to subject them to his rule. He was, however, an ardent admirer of Greek culture and treated them leniently, leaving them to rule themselves as long as they paid him tribute and did not become too independent. Cyrus the Great was a very different conqueror. When he marched against Lydia he invited the Ionian cities to revolt against Croesus. They refused. So, when he had conquered Croesus, he sent his generals to lay siege to the Ionian cities, one by one. Two of the cities put all their citizens on board their ships and sailed off to settle in new lands in the Aegean sea. The rest had to pay tribute to Cyrus and contribute warships to his navy and hoplites to his army whenever he demanded them, and put up with the rulers he chose for them. The same fate befell the more recent colonies which had been founded on the Bosphorus and the southern coast of the Black Sea.

(b) The Ionian Revolt

Just under 50 years after they had been conquered by Cyrus the Ionian city-states revolted against Persia and drove out the rulers imposed on them. This occurred when Darius had become King of Persia and was planning to enlarge his empire. The last thing he was prepared to allow was a successful revolt. Nevertheless the Ionians held out for five years despite their inability, after generations of rivalry, to co-operate under a unified command. In the decisive sea-battle, off the island of Lade, two of the largest Ionian naval contingents deserted. Although the others fought well and skilfully they were hopelessly outnumbered. Miletus, the city-state which had begun the revolt, was besieged and captured and the inhabitants deported to live beside the Persian Gulf.

There had been one incident at the beginning of the revolt which was bound to have consequences. An Ionian army, supported by contingents from Athens and the small city-state of Eretria, marched inland and burnt Sardis. Sardis, since its capture by Cyrus, had become the capital of the Persian Empire in the west. Darius was not a ruler to forgive such an insult to his empire, and he had reason to consider the Athenian participation as an act of treachery. Some ten years earlier Athenian envoys, with a view to enlisting Persian help against an expected attack by Sparta, had given earth and water to the Governor of Sardis as the representative of Darius. By this they had acknowledged Persian suzerainty. The envoys were censured on their return to Athens, but in Persian eyes the relationship could not be so easily revoked.

(c) The Marathon campaign

In 490 BC, five years after the Battle of Lade, Darius was ready to exact vengeance for the burning of his western capital. He sent a seaborn expedition across the Aegean Sea, capturing islands as it went. Eretria on the Island of Euboea, opposite the northern shore of Attica, was captured with help from traitors within the walls. It was sacked and its inhabitants deported to Media. (Later Plato wrote a short poem in the form of an epitaph for the Eretrians which went thus:

> Though we are Eretrians, yet we are buried here, far from the thunder of the Aegean Sea, in the landlocked plain of Ecbatana. To Eretria, once our famous homeland, to Athens, near neighbour to Euboea, and to our beloved sea, hail and farewell!

By the fifth century the sea had become so much a part of the lives of Greeks that the pathos of the Eretrians' situation lay in the unbearable distance of Ecbatana from the sea).

After sacking Eretria the Persian expeditionary force was landed on the Attic coast, beside the Bay of Marathon. Here was a flat area of shoreland (suitable for the Persian cavalry) encircled by steep mountains. Both sides waited, the Persians by their ships on the shore, the Athenians (who had marched out from Athens to meet them) at the foot of the mountains. The Athenians had been promised help by the Spartans as soon as they had finished celebrating a very important religious festival. They came too late, but help did come from the little city of Plataea, a neighbour and ally of the Athenians. They sent their entire citizen army of 1,000 hoplites, for which the Athenians were grateful ever after. For several days there was stalemate as the Athenians dared not advance far into the plains for fear of the Persian cavalry, while their own position was too strong for the Persians to attack.

After some days the Athenian generals received a message from some Ionian soldiers (who had been conscripted into the Persian army) that the Persian cavalry were out of the way. (Where they had gone is a matter of dispute among historians.) The Athenians attacked at once, charging at the double, and, thanks to the brilliant tactics of their general Miltiades, broke the Persians' line, driving them back to their ships with the loss of 6,400 of their men.

> As the Persians fled, the Greeks pursued, cutting them down, until they reached the sea. Then calling for fire they began to take hold of the ships. In the ensuing struggle the senior general, Kallimakhos, was killed fighting bravely, as was another general, Stesilaos. Kynegeiros also fell. His hand was cut off with an axe as he took hold of the stern of a ship. Other famous Athenians fell too; nevertheless seven ships were captured.
>
> (HERODOTUS, 6.114)

The Athenians, although outnumbered in the battle, only lost 192 men. It was a triumph of the arms and armour, the discipline and the infantry tactics, of the Athenians and Plataeans.

It was a glorious victory and a great boost to the morale of the Greeks to learn that the Persians were far from invincible. But only a fraction of the Great King's forces had been engaged. He had been twice humiliated, once at Sardis and now at Marathon. No one can have doubted that the Persians would be back, and next time it would not be a mere fraction of the Great King's forces that the Greeks would have to face.

(d) A reprieve

There was, however, a ten-year reprieve. Three years after Marathon, when Darius was engaged in training and equipping his grand army for a full-scale land invasion, the province of Egypt revolted from his empire. Before Darius could deal with the Egyptians he died. His son Xerxes had to suppress the Egyptian revolt, and then two more revolts in Babylon before he could turn his attention to the Greeks.

The Athenians used their respite well. They discovered a very rich deposit of silver in the state-owned silver mine at Mount Laurium in southern Attica, and they were persuaded by Themistocles to spend it on a crash programme of warship building. 300 triremes were constructed and crews trained to man them. Meanwhile Xerxes was making his own preparations.

Recapitulation

Before recounting Xerxes's invasion, it might be helpful to summarise the relevant history of the preceding centuries.

Some time about 1,000 BC the Ionians fled from Greece and founded their colonies on the Aegean Coast of Asia Minor. At this time the ancestors of the Persians were probably still moving westwards, with their flocks of sheep and cattle, from eastern Iran to the western edge of the Zagros Mountains where they settled.

Some time about 700 BC a new dynasty of Lydian kings began to threaten the Ionian cities. At this time the Assyrians were dominating the lands in and around Mesopotamia, including the Iranian tribes of Media. By the end of the seventh century the Medes had formed a strong kingdom and in 612 BC, in alliance with the Babylonians, they overthrew the Assyrian Empire.

About 560 BC Croesus conquered the Ionian cities. A few years later Cyrus the Great overthrew the King of the Medes and became ruler of Medes and Persians. Not many years later he defeated and captured Croesus and conquered the Ionian cities. Thereafter he conquered Babylon, gaining control of the Babylonian Empire, which stretched from Cilicia to the borders of Egypt and included Syria and all of Mesopotamia. At some time he probably added to his empire the lands to the east of the Iranian Plateau (i.e. modern Afghanistan and the lands to the north-east of it).

In 530 BC Cyrus was killed fighting tribes to the north-east of his empire and was succeeded by his son Cambyses.

In 525 BC Cambyses conquered Egypt and added it to the empire.

In 522 BC Cambyses died on the way back from Egypt after an 'impostor' had seized the throne in Persis. In the same year Darius with six other conspirators killed the 'impostor' and Darius became king.

Between 522 BC and 500 BC Darius conquered the north-western corner of India and, in the west, added to his Empire Samos, Lesbos and Chios, (Greek islands off the coast of Asia Minor). Then he crossed the Bosphorus into Europe by a boat-bridge (supplied by his Ionian Greek subjects), marched north, crossed the Danube by another boat-bridge and tried unsuccessfully to defeat the Scythians of the steppes. He and his generals did, however, extend the Empire's frontiers to the Danube incorporating in it all of Thrace. He also received the submission of the King of Macedon (in northern Greece) whose sister then married a Persian noble.

In 499 BC occurred the Ionian Revolt and the burning of Sardis by Ionians, Athenians and Eretrians.

By 494 BC the Ionian Revolt was suppressed.

In 490 BC the expedition, sent by Darius to avenge the burning of Sardis, sacked Eretria but was defeated by the Athenians and Plataeans at Marathon.

In 486 BC, while Darius was planning to lead a much bigger expedition, Egypt revolted and Darius died.

Between 486 and 480 BC Darius' successor Xerxes put down the revolt in Egypt and another revolt in Babylon, and continued the preparations for the great Greek expedition.

Chapter 4
The Great Expedition: the First Stages

Xerxes' preparations

Napoleon said that an army marches on its stomach. The army that Xerxes was proposing to bring to Greece had a very large stomach. For half of the distance from the Hellespont to Athens the army would be marching through territory which had been brought under Persian control twelve years earlier by Darius' son-in-law Mardonius. Xerxes sent agents to organise dumps of food at four places along this part of the route. More food was to be ready to feed his troops when they got to Macedon, whose king, Alexander, sympathised with the Greeks but would be quickly eliminated if he tried to oppose Xerxes.

During Mardonius' campaign a Persian fleet had been wrecked by a storm while rounding the headland of Mount Athos, so a canal was dug across the neck of the promontory.

Darius had used a bridge of boats to take his army across the Bosphorus and again across the Danube. Xerxes wanted two bridges of boats to take his army across the Dardanelles. For these bridges cables of flax were woven by the Phoenicians, and of papyrus reed by the Egyptians. With some of these cables 360 boats were lashed together to make a crossing for the infantry and cavalry. With the others 314 boats were lashed together further downstream for the baggage animals, non-combatant troops and camp followers. Planks were laid across the bridges and covered with trampled earth for the soldiers to march on, and on the bridge intended for the animals hedges were placed along the sides to give them confidence.

> When the bridges were completed a great storm arose and utterly destroyed them. When Xerxes learnt of this he was furious and gave orders that the Hellespont should be scourged with a hundred lashes and have fetters dropped into it...The men who inflicted the lashes were to utter the following arrogant words: 'Malignant river, your master punishes you thus for your unprovoked wickedness. King Xerxes shall cross you whether you wish it or not.'
>
> (HERODOTUS, 7.34,35)

Then Xerxes executed those responsible for building the bridges, appointed new engineers and had the bridges rebuilt with improved cables.

Contingents of troops from all the provinces were ordered to meet Xerxes on his march from Mesopotamia to Sardis, where he spent the winter of 481-480 BC.

During the winter heralds were sent to the Greek states to demand earth and water as token of surrender. However heralds were not sent to Athens and Sparta. When, previously, Darius had sent heralds to Athens and Sparta they had not come back. The Athenians had thrown the heralds who came to Athens into a pit and the Spartans had thrown the heralds who came to Sparta into a well. The Athenians told the heralds to get their earth from the pit and the Spartans told them to get their water from the well. But heralds were supposed to be under the protection of the gods and the Spartans ever after had a bad conscience about what they had done. Some years later they tried to atone for their offence, but that is another, curious, story (to be found in chapters 134-7 of Book VII of Herodotus' *History*). Herodotus reports no evidence that the Athenians either repented or suffered retribution for their mistreatment of the heralds.

The Delphic Oracle

The Greeks who had decided to fight made an oath that those Greek cities which voluntarily surrendered to the Persians should, when the crisis was over, be made to pay one tenth of their wealth to the Delphic temple. Perhaps they hoped this would persuade the Delphic Oracle to encourage other Greeks to resist. If so, they hoped in vain. All those who went to the oracle to ask what they should do when Xerxes began his invasion were given an answer that predicted – or seemed to predict (the answers of the Oracle were never *absolutely* clear) – that resistance was doomed to failure.

At about this time the Greeks invented a new word – 'to medise': meaning to side with the Persian enemy (to the Greeks the Medes and the Persians were the same people).* Not long before Xerxes' invasion the reputation of the Delphic Oracle had been damaged by

---

* In the crisis of 1940 a new word 'quisling' was invented. It was the name of a Norwegian politician who sided with the German invaders of Norway, so 'quisling' and 'mediser' have a similar meaning.

more than one bribery scandal, but Greeks – and foreigners – still paid attention to its answers, since they were supposed to be inspired by the God Apollo. It must therefore have been very discouraging to patriotic Greeks to find that the Oracle – or the God Apollo himself – had 'medised'.

The preparations of the Greeks

In the autumn of 481 BC representatives of the states which had decided to fight the Persians met at Sparta. They swore alliance, agreed to end all hostilities among themselves and chose the Spartans to command all their forces both on land and at sea. They sent envoys to Corfu, Crete and Sicily to ask for help from the Greeks there, and they sent spies to Persia to spy out Xerxes' preparations. The spies were captured and, on Xerxes' instructions, were not executed but shown everything there was to see and then sent back home to frighten the Greeks (so Xerxes expected) by telling them about his irresistible army. The envoys sent to Corfu, Crete and Sicily returned to report that there was no help to be expected from any of those islands.

In the spring of 480 BC a second meeting was held, this time at the Isthmus of Corinth. 31 states were represented and together they could count on providing 40,000 heavy-armed infantry and 70,000 light-armed infantry. Their only cavalry was the cavalry of Thessaly which could not be relied on unless Xerxes could be stopped before he reached the Thessalian plains. At sea they had 400 warships.

Xerxes sets off to war

Herodotus has described the departure from Sardis of Xerxes' Grand Army thus:

> First came the porters with the pack animals, and after them, without intervals, came the great mass of troops from many nations. When rather more than half of the host had passed, a gap was left to separate these from the king. The royal guard was led by an elite regiment of 1,000 cavalry. They were followed by 1,000 spearmen, also an elite formation, who carried their spears pointed downwards. Next came ten sacred horses of the breed known as Nisaean, splendidly caparisoned (these horses are very large and bred in the extensive plain of Nisaea in Media). After the ten horses came the sacred chariot of the god

[Ahura-Mazda], drawn by eight white horses. Behind it came Xerxes riding in a chariot drawn by Nisaean horses. Beside him rode his charioteer, a Persian named Patiramphes, son of Otanes.

So Xerxes rode out of Sardis and, from time to time, when he was tired of his chariot, he rode in a coach instead. Behind him came 1,000 spearmen, all Persian noblemen of the highest rank, holding their spears in the normal manner. After them marched another thousand picked Persian horsemen and then 10,000 infantry, chosen from the rest of the Persians. 1,000 of these had golden pomegranates on the butts of their spears and enclosed the other 9,000 who had silver pomegranates. (The spearmen who marched in front of Xerxes with their spears pointed to the ground also had golden pomegranates, and those who followed closest behind Xerxes had golden apples.) Next in the order of march came ten thousand Persian cavalry. Then there was a gap of half a mile before the rest of Xerxes' host followed hugger mugger.

(HERODOTUS, 7.40,41)

The odds

According to Herodotus, Xerxes brought to Greece 2,317,610 fighting men, an equal number of non-combatant troops and innumerable camp followers (he mentions eunuchs and concubines and women to make bread). Herodotus gives the overall figure of 3,000 for the ships in Xerxes' armada, 1,207 being warships, the rest transports to keep the land forces supplied with food. When the crews of the ships (including the Ionian Greeks who were serving under compulsion) and the marines (who were mostly Persians) were added to the land forces, Herodotus made the total of Xerxes' manpower to be more than 5 million. Modern historians usually divide this figure by about ten. Even so the Persians' success in keeping more than 500,000 human beings, and their animals, fed and on the move through the rugged countryside of Greece shows a very high level of organising ability.

Such a massive superiority in numbers was, however, not all gain. It made it necessary for the army and the fleet to move more or less at the same pace and to keep in close contact so that the transports could feed the army, the warships could protect the transports and the army could protect the anchorages of the warships. In these circumstances the leaders of the Greeks saw that the one strategy that held out some hope of success was to hold a line where both the Persian army and the Persian navy would have to fight in such a confined space that their superior numbers would be more hindrance than help. If this could be brought about, the superior skill and equipment of the Greek heavy-armed infantry (which had been demonstrated at Marathon) might prove decisive on land, and the more heavily built warships of the Athenians might be able to defeat the swifter Phoenician ships of the Persian navy, encumbered as they might be by all the other contingents that Xerxes had brought with him.

The first choice of the Greek generals – the Vale of Tempe in the north of Thessaly – turned out to be a mistake, as it would have been possible for Xerxes' army to by-pass the position. So they withdrew: whereupon the Thessalians with their cavalry promptly 'medised'. Instead it was decided to send a small force commanded by Leonidas, one of the two Spartan kings, to hold the pass of Thermopylae while the Greek fleet took up a position beside the straits at the north end of the island of Euboea. Leonidas' force consisted of 300 full Spartan citizens and about 5,000 other troops, mainly allies of the Spartans from the Peloponnese. The fleet of some 280 warships was under the command of a Spartan admiral. This had been agreed at the meeting at Sparta, although more than half of the ships and crews were supplied by Athens.

Thermopylae and Artemisium

(a) The site

Herodotus describes the positions which the Greeks had chosen to occupy:

> This is what the two places are like. At Artemisium the sea is no more than a narrow channel between the island of Skiathos and the mainland. This channel leads to the tip of the island of Euboea where there is a temple of Artemis.
>
> As for Thermopylae, this is where the pass into Greece is at its narrowest – only 50 yards wide. But the narrowest parts of all are just before you get to Thermopylae and just behind it. In both of these places there is only room for one cart to pass at a time. West of Thermopylae there is a high, sheer mountain that cannot be climbed. On the east side there is sea and marsh.

[Herodotus seems to have visited Thermopylae on a cloudy day and for lack of a compass – still uninvented – to have got his directions wholly wrong. He should have said 'south' and 'north' not 'west' and 'east'.]

> At the entrance to the pass a wall had been built. At one time there had been gates in it...This wall was so old that most of it had fallen down. The Greeks decided to rebuild it and to make their stand there. There is a village very near the road and from this village they intended to get their supplies.
>
> (HERODOTUS, 7.176)

(b) The first skirmish
By this time Xerxes had reached Therma (today it is called Salonika) on the coast of Macedonia. His fleet was ordered to make its way along the coast to the safe haven of the Gulf of Pagasae. To reach it they would have to pass the Greek ships at Artemisium. Ahead of his main fleet Xerxes sent his ten fastest ships. These found three Greek ships stationed off Skiathos to keep watch. On seeing the ten ships the Greek ships fled as fast as they could. One of them (an Athenian ship) rowed fast enough to reach the mouth of the Peneus river, where the crew beached their ship and escaped back to Athens overland. The other two were not so lucky.

> The Troizenian ship was quickly captured, and the Persians took the handsomest of the marines who were on board and sacrificed him on the prow of the ship. They thought it was a sign of good luck that the first Greek they captured was so handsome. The third ship (from the island of Aegina) gave them some trouble owing to the heroism of one of its marines named Pytheas. When the ship was captured he went on fighting until he was completely slashed to pieces. When the Persians found that, though fallen, he was still breathing, they made a great effort to keep him alive because of his bravery. Treating his wounds with myrrh and binding them up with linen bandages, they took him back to their camp. There they showed him off to the whole army, praising him and treating him well. But they made slaves of the others they had captured in his ship.
>
> (HERODOTUS, 7.180,181)

The Greek crews waiting at Artemisium were quickly informed

about what had happened to their three ships by fire signals from the island of Skiathos. In alarm they withdrew into the channel between Euboea and the mainland. Meanwhile three of the ten ships from the Persian fleet searched out a reef (which they had been warned about) in the middle of the channel. When they had located it they fixed a stone pillar to mark it. Then they signalled to the main fleet that the way was clear to the Gulf of Pagasae.

(c) The storm

Xerxes' fleet did not reach the gulf on its first day of sailing, and had to spend the night beside an open shore. The first ships to arrive were moored to the beach but those which could not find room anchored off shore, eight deep, facing towards the sea. Next morning...

> day broke clear and windless, but soon the sea was whipped up into a violent storm by a strong easterly wind (known locally as a 'hellespontias'). Some of the sailors whose ships were moored to the shore had noticed the wind getting up. They pulled their ships onto the beach in good time and so saved themselves and their ships; but the ships which were caught at sea were scattered. Some were cast up onto the shore, some dashed against rocks known as 'The Ovens' at the foot of Mount Pelion, others against Cape Sepias itself or at various places along the coast... In this disaster at least four hundred ships were lost, innumerable men and a vast amount of treasure. This provided a windfall for a local landowner since in the course of time many gold and silver drinking vessels were washed ashore. He found Persian treasure chests and other valuables and became a very rich man – not that this saved him from misfortune, as he suffered some tragedy connected with the death of a son.
>
> (HERODOTUS, 7.188,189)

This storm had done no harm to the Greek fleet which had been sheltering behind the island of Euboea. Not surprisingly the Greeks saw it – just as the Elizabethans saw the storms that scattered the Spanish Armada – as divine intervention. In one of the Greek myths Boreas (the god of the north wind) carried off Orithyia, daughter of the King of Athens, to be his wife, so the Athenians felt that they had a special relationship with him. They had prayed for his help and he had given it. So when they got back to Athens, they built him a temple. On the other side the Persians had heard that the coast round Cape Sepias was sacred to the sea goddess Thetis, because Thetis had been kidnapped there by Peleus to be *his* wife. So their priests, the Magi, made sacrifices to Thetis and her sisters, the Nereid sea nymphs, and so calmed the storm on the fourth day. 'Or perhaps it abated of its own accord,' wrote Herodotus, who did not feel obliged to believe everything he recorded.

(d) A Persian mistake

When the Greek fleet withdrew behind the island of Euboea, they had left look-outs on the heights above Artemisium. These quickly came to the Greek fleet to report the storm and its effect on the Persian fleet. The Greeks sacrificed in gratitude to Poseidon and returned to their station off Artemisium. At about the same time the depleted, but still huge, Persian fleet put out to sea, and safely rounded Cape Sepias to arrive in the security of the Gulf of Pagasae – all except for a squadron of 15 ships which were late in putting out to sea. These mistook the Greek ships at Artemisium for their own.

> They were commanded by Sandoces, the son of Thamasios, the Governor of Cyme in Aeolia. He had formerly been one of the royal judges, but had been condemned to be crucified by King Darius because he had taken a bribe to give an unjust verdict. While Sandoces was actually hanging on the cross, Darius decided that he had done more good than harm to the royal family, and that he, Darius, had been more hasty than wise. So he had him released. In this way Sandoces escaped being put to death by Darius, but he did not escape a second time when he sailed into the middle of the Greeks. The Greeks saw the ships coming and realised the mistake they had made. Sailing up to them they easily captured them.
>
> (HERODOTUS, 7.194)

In the meantime Xerxes had led his army through Thessaly to encamp a few miles from the pass of Thermopylae. So the hostile forces were in position for the first battles of the war. The battles would take place in situations chosen by the Greeks. The huge Persian forces would be obliged to fight on land in a narrow pass and at sea in a narrow strait. Only one thing was lacking: the Greeks had not committed an adequate force for the defence of Thermopylae.

Chapter 5
The Battles: Thermopylae and Artemisium

The Spartans had reassured the cities of Central Greece by saying that Leonidas' army was merely an advance guard and that the main part of the Spartan army would be setting out to reinforce it as soon as they had finished holding a sacred festival – the same festival that had prevented their arrival at Marathon in time for the battle. Whether they ever really intended to send their main army so far north of their main defensive position at the Isthmus of Corinth is doubtful. Leonidas had chosen his 300 Spartiates (full Spartan citizens) from among men who already had children, which suggests that he did not expect many of them to return home.

The arrival of Xerxes at Thermopylae

After reporting the first naval skirmishes Herodotus turns his attention to events on land:

> Meanwhile Xerxes marched with his army through Thessaly. On the third day he came to the land of the Malians...He encamped there, opposite Leonidas' army which was stationed in the pass of Thermopylae...When the Persians approached the pass, the Greeks were alarmed. They argued whether they should stay or retreat. The soldiers who had come from Southern Greece wanted to march south to defend the Isthmus of Corinth, but the soldiers from cities in Central Greece were angry at this proposal. Seeing this, Leonidas made the decision to remain there, and to send messengers round the cities asking for help. The messengers were to tell the cities that there were not enough men with Leonidas to halt the Persian army.

The scout

> While the Greeks were making up their minds to stay, Xerxes sent a horseman to scout ahead and report to him

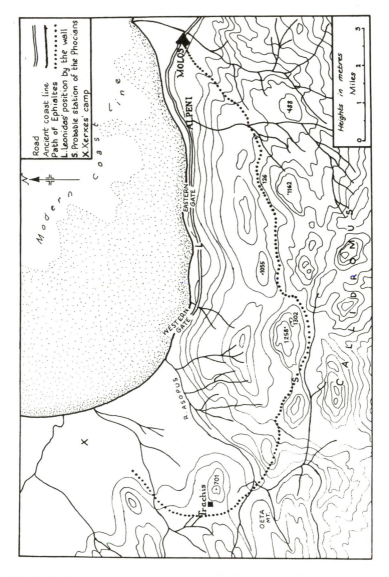

Fig. 9. The Battle of Thermopylae (after N.G.L. Hammond).

how many Greeks were there and what they were doing. He had heard that a small army was encamped there, led by some Spartans under the command of King Leonidas, who was a descendant of Herakles. When the horseman rode towards the camp he could not see the whole force. This was because part of it was stationed inside the wall (which they had rebuilt and were guarding). What he could see was the troops who had taken up their position outside the wall. These happened to be Spartans at the time of his mission. Some of them were exercising themselves and others were combing their hair. This amazed the scout but he duly counted them. After carefully noting everything, he rode back without haste – for no one pursued him, or indeed took any notice of him at all. Going to Xerxes he told him everything he had seen.

When Xerxes heard what the scout had to say he could not grasp the fact that the Spartans were preparing to die, and to kill while they had strength to do so. He thought their behaviour was absurd and sent for Demaratos [the exiled king of Sparta], who was in his camp.

When Demaratos came, Xerxes questioned him, wishing to learn what the Spartans were doing.

"I have already been laughed at by you," said Demaratos, "when we set out for Greece, because I told you about these men, and how things would turn out. I want most of all to tell you the truth. Listen to me again. These men have come to fight us for the pass, and that is what they are preparing to do. It is their custom, when they are about to risk their lives, to make their hair elegant. This you must understand. If you conquer these men, and the others who have remained in Sparta, no other race of men will dare to oppose you. For you are about to attack the bravest men from the finest kingdom in Greece."

(HERODOTUS, 7.196, 207, 208, 209)

The fight for the pass

Xerxes did not believe what ex-King Demaratos told him. Demaratos, however, knew his own countrymen.

All through one day the Persian army attacked the Greeks, but the Greeks drove them back each time. The pass was too narrow for their immense superiority in numbers to be of much use to the Persians. The Greeks had longer spears and better armour and, according to Herodotus, the Spartans fought with great skill. Very many Persians were killed, including many of the royal guard. The next day the Persians tried again, but with no better success. Leonidas had divided the Greeks into several companies, so that, while some companies fought, the others could rest and get ready to fight again.

The traitor

When the Persians found that everything was the same as it had been the day before, they retreated again. Xerxes wondered what to do. Then a Malian named Ephialtes came to him, hoping to earn a great reward. He told Xerxes that there was a track through the mountains to Thermopylae. By telling Xerxes this he caused the deaths of all the Greeks who stayed to defend the pass. Xerxes was delighted with Ephialtes and sent Hydarnes and his men to go with him.

(HERODOTUS,7.212,213)

[Hydarnes commanded the royal guard. They were known as 'The Immortals' because there were always 10,000 of them, never less. Whenever any one of them became a casualty, there was always another guardsman designated to take his place.]

The Persians' night march

The Immortals set out from their camp at dusk...Leaving the Asopos river they marched all night, keeping Mount Oeta on their right and the mountains of Trachis on their left. When day broke they were at the top of the mountain. This part of the mountain, as has already been mentioned, was guarded by a thousand Phokian infantry, defending both their own country and the pass, just as they had promised Leonidas. The Persians reached the top of the pass unobserved as they had been hidden by a forest of oak trees which covered the mountain; and even then the Phokians became aware of them only because it was a windless night and the fallen leaves naturally made a great noise under the feet of the Persians. The Phokians hearing this noise had just enough time to jump up and put on their armour as the Persians arrived. The Persians were amazed to see men arming themselves, for they had counted on meeting with no opposition and here was an army.

Hydarnes was frightened that the Phokians might be Spartans, and asked Ephialtes whose army it was. When Ephialtes told him, he drew up his Persians in full battle formation. The Phokians were struck by a hail of arrows and fled to the peak of the mountain. They thought that the Persians had come to attack them, and prepared to die. But the Persians with Ephialtes and Hydarnes left them alone and hurried on down the mountainside.

(HERODOTUS,7.215,217,218)

The news reaches Leonidas

The Greeks at Thermopylae were first told of the death that awaited them that morning by the prophet Megistias, who had inspected the sacrifices. Then came deserters to tell them that the Persians were on their way to take them in the rear. This news reached them while it was still night time. Finally, after day had dawned, they had the information for the third time, from look-outs who scrambled down the cliffside from the mountain above.

(HERODOTUS, 7.219)

The council of war

So the Greeks held a council of war. Some said they must not abandon the pass, while others thought they should. In the end they split into two groups. Some prepared to remain with Leonidas, others began to march away to their own cities. Some people say that Leonidas himself told them to depart because he did not want them all to be killed. He himself and his 300 Spartans could not march away from a pass they had come to defend without bringing disgrace on themselves. I think that Leonidas saw that the allies were not keen to stay and face the Persians with him, and so ordered them to march away. But he himself could not retreat without dishonour.

(HERODOTUS, 7.219,220)

At this point in his narrative he recalls that at the beginning of the war the Delphic priestess had given an oracle to the Spartans, in the usual roundabout language, which implied that either Sparta must be sacked by the Persians or else lose one of her kings. Herodotus gives his opinion that Leonidas had this oracle in mind and wished to win glory exclusively for the Spartans and for this reason dismissed the allied forces, who did not, he thinks, go off in disorder after an argument.

> I consider my opinion is confirmed by this. He dismissed Megistias, so that he should not die with him.

[Megistias (though not a Spartan) was the army's prophet, and it was he who had foretold what was about to happen to them when he inspected the sacrifices that morning.]

> Though he was dismissed, Megistias did not leave. He merely sent away his son who was soldiering with him and who was his only child.
> After the departure of the allies in accordance with Leonidas' orders, only the Thebans and the Thespians were left. The Thebans remained against their will, kept by Leonidas as hostages, but the Thespians volunteered to stay, refusing to abandon Leonidas and his Spartans. They stayed and died with them. They were commanded by their general Demophilos.
>
> (HERODOTUS, 7.221,222)

The final battle

> At sunrise Xerxes made drink offerings to the gods, and then waited until the hour when the market place begins to fill [between 9 and 10 a.m.]. Then he attacked. He did this on the advice of Ephialtes, as the path down the mountains is shorter and more direct than the circuitous way up. So he had worked out that the Immortals would be behind Leonidas' army by this time.
> Xerxes' Persians then advanced and Leonidas and the Greeks marched out further than before, into the broader part of the pass, intending to fight until they died. Previously they had fought in the narrow part.
> Very large numbers of the Persians were killed, for their officers were flogging them on from behind. Many of them fell into the sea and were drowned. Many more were trampled to death by their own men. No one gave a thought to the dying. The Greeks fought recklessly and with all the strength they had, since they knew that they were certain to be killed by those Persians who had come over the

mountains behind them. By now most of them had broken their spears and were killing Persians with their swords.

Leonidas, fighting with the utmost bravery, was killed at this stage of the battle, and with him other important Spartans...Many eminent Persians were also killed, including two half-brothers of Xerxes. There was a fierce fight for the corpse of Leonidas, and it was in this fight that the half-brothers of Xerxes were killed. Finally the Greeks outfought the Persians and rescued their King's body, routing the Persians four times.

(HERODOTUS, 7.223,224,225)

The end

So the battle raged until the troops guided by Ephialtes came up. When the Greeks learnt that they had come, the fighting took a different form. The Greeks retreated to the narrow part of the pass and, going beyond the wall, they all – except the Thebans – took up their position together on the mound. This mound is at the entrance to the pass, where there is now a stone lion erected to the memory of Leonidas. Here the Greeks defended themselves with daggers – those who still had them – or with their hands and teeth, until the Persians, who had knocked down the wall and were attacking them from all sides, buried them beneath a hail of missiles.

(HERODOTUS, 7.225)

Herodotus admired the heroes of Thermopylae so much that he found out the names of all the Spartans who fought and died there. He particularly admired the Spartan who refused to be impressed when a local inhabitant came up to tell him that there was such a multitude of Persians that when they shot their arrows the sun would be eclipsed. 'That', he said, 'is good news, as we will be able to fight in the shade.'

The epitaphs

After the war a memorial was set up at Thermopylae with an inscription which said:

On this spot 4,000 Greeks once fought against three millions.

The Spartans had a special inscription which asked anyone who passed by to

> tell the Spartans that their orders were obeyed and Leonidas and his three hundred Spartiates are still occupying the pass.

And there was a special inscription for Megistias, written by a poet who was a friend of his. It said:

> This is a memorial to the famous Megistias, killed by the Persians. He was a prophet, and he knew quite well what was about to happen, but he could not bring himself to desert the Spartan commanders.

The withdrawal from Artemisium

During the days of fighting at Thermopylae there had been two battles off Artemisium in which the outnumbered Greek fleet had received a battering but had held its own. There had also been another storm which had wrecked a Persian squadron of two hundred ships as it sailed round the east coast of Euboea to take the Greeks in the rear.

The Greek commanders had arranged for a fast ship to be standing ready at Thermopylae and another at Artemisium to carry news of any disaster to either fleet or army. In this way the commanders of the fleet learnt that Leonidas was dead and the Persian army free to advance into central Greece. They therefore gave orders for the fleet to withdraw to Salamis, the island close to the mainland of Attica and not far from the harbours of Athens. The Athenian admiral Themistocles, as he sailed south, left graffiti carved on the rocks at places where sailors of the Persian fleet might come ashore to get water, urging them, if they were Greeks from Ionia or Caria, to desert, or at least to fight half-heartedly for the Persians.

Chapter 6
The Battles: Salamis and Plataea

Athens abandoned

Nothing could now save Athens. The Athenian Assembly had passed a decree that the women and children were to be sent away to the city-state of Troizen in the Peloponnese, where they were given a generous welcome. Many had left, but others had stayed or come back in the hope that the Persians would not come. Now there was a panic evacuation. It is described by the biographer and moralist Plutarch in his life of Themistocles. Plutarch wrote his biographies nearly five hundred years after the Battle of Salamis, but it is reasonable to suppose that he drew on contemporary accounts which have long since perished.

> All Athens put out to sea. It was a sight which aroused pity in some and in others amazement that they could be doing anything so drastic as sending their families away to Troizen and themselves crossing over to Salamis, paying no attention to the tears and lamentations of their parents. Saddest of all was the fate of the very old who had to be left behind, and of the family pets which showed their affection towards their masters by running beside them, howling pitifully, as they embarked. It is said that a dog belonging to Xanthippos, the father of Pericles, could not bear to be left behind, so it leaped into the sea and tried to swim across the straits beside its master's trireme. It reached the shore at Salamis, where it collapsed and died. It was buried there and the grave gives its name to the place that is still called Kynossema – that is to say, the tomb of the dog.
>
> (PLUTARCH, Life of Themistocles, 10)

The Persians in Athens

All the Athenian men of military age either went on board the fleet, which was stationed in Salamis Bay, or took up positions guarding the shores of Salamis.

Nine days after the disaster of Thermopylae the Persians entered Attica, burning the villages as they came, and, soon afterwards, the Persian fleet sailed round the coast and into Phaleron Bay, which was then the main harbour of Athens.

Not quite all the Athenian men of military age had embarked. A few Athenians, who from extreme poverty or because they had duties connected with the temple, had decided to stay. These men fortified the Acropolis with a wooden palisade (wooden, because the Delphic priestess had said that all the Athenian territory would be captured except for the wooden wall. Themistocles, never at a loss, had persuaded most of the Athenians – but not the literal-minded – that 'wooden wall' meant their ships). The defenders fought desperately and with resource. When the Persians burnt down their wooden wall with flaming arrows they kept them off by rolling rocks down onto them. Finally the Persians found a precipitous and unguarded path, made their way to the top and massacred all the defenders who did not commit suicide by jumping off the rock. Then, as a punishment for the burning of Sardis, they burnt the temple of Athena and all the other shrines on the Acropolis.

Dissension in the Greek fleet

The sight of the Acropolis going up in flames had such a demoralising effect on the commanders of the naval contingents that they all but hoisted sail and set course for the Isthmus or their own home ports. They would have done so had not Themistocles argued again and again that it would be disastrous to lose their one opportunity of a naval battle in circumstances which gave them an advantage over the Persians. Finally he had to use the threat to remove the 200 Athenian ships and their crews, put on board their families and sail away to the west to found another city, just as the inhabitants of the little city of Phokaia had done when Cyrus first conquered Ionia. This would make the Greek fleet too weak to fight the Persians at the Isthmus or anywhere else. Themistocles' final ploy was to send a trusted slave with a message to Xerxes. He was to say: Themistocles had turned traitor and wanted to help Xerxes; the Greek fleet was about to sail away; the commanders were quarrelling with one another; if the Persians attacked at once they would win a splendid victory. The ruse worked. Xerxes gave his orders. Persian troops were to be landed under cover of darkness on the little island of Psyttaleia to assist any Persian crews – and kill any Greeks – who might become stranded

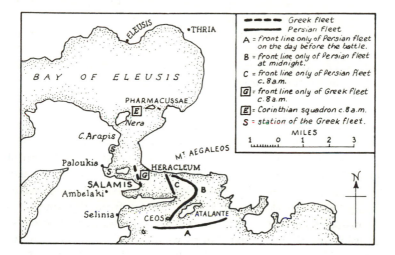

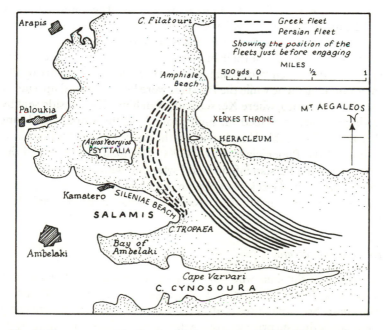

Fig. 10. *Two stages of the Battle of Salamis (after N.G.L. Hammond).*

there. The main Persian fleet was to put to sea that night to catch the Greeks as they tried to escape, while the Egyptian squadron was to sail round Salamis to take them in the rear.

News of these preparations was brought by a ship from the Ionian island of Tenos which deserted to the Greeks. This settled matters. The Greek commanders drew up their order of battle for the next day and rested their crews for the night.

The battle

When the Greeks had not appeared by dawn, the Persian fleet rowed into the straits between the island of Salamis and the mainland of Attica. They found the Greek ships waiting for them. As the Persian fleet approached, the Greeks backed water to lead the Persians further in. Then the dawn breeze got up from the south (as Themistocles knew it would), started a swell and helped to cause confusion among the Persians' ships, which stood higher in the water than the Greek ships, and were already crowded too closely together. At that point the Greeks attacked. Their favourite tactics, in which they had been well drilled, were to charge the enemy vessels amidships and hole them with the bronze-covered rams that projected from their prows. The Persians relied more on the fire-power of the archers they carried on their higher and more extensive decks. The Greeks had manoeuvred so that they had sea-room enough to execute their ramming tactic while the Persians were being pressed up against the shore of Attica, where Xerxes had given himself a ringside seat by having his throne placed on high ground on the slopes of Mount Aegaleos. This enabled him to witness the destruction of his best ships – those of the Phoenicians – by the 200 Athenian triremes, and the slaughter of the Persian infantry on Psyttaleia (who found themselves to *the rear* of the Greek fleet) by an Athenian general who spotted them from Salamis and took across a force large enough to annihilate them.

Eye-witness account

Among the Athenians who participated in the battle of Salamis was Aeschylus, a poet and writer of tragedies, a veteran of the Battle of Marathon. Some eight years after the battle he did a surprising thing – not altogether surprising to the Athenians as it had been done twice before, but it was never done again. Instead of writing a play about mythical or legendary characters, as was the custom, he wrote a play about the Battle of Salamis. Furthermore he told the story from the viewpoint of the Persians – that is to say the play takes place in Persia, outside the royal palace at Susa and near the tomb of Darius: the battle is reported by Persians to Persians; and it is Persians who react to the news and comment on it. On the other hand into the mouths of these 'Persians' are put sentiments that contrive to be highly flattering to the Greeks (especially to the Athenians), are Greek in tone, and express a Greek moral – that the Gods hate excess of prosperity and are inexorable in punishing impiety and arrogance.

The characters are a chorus of elderly Persians who are acting as a sort of Council of State in Xerxes' absence; Atossa, the mother of Xerxes and widow of Darius; a messenger; and the ghost of Darius. Towards the end of the play Xerxes himself appears, in great distress.

Obviously it is not a realistic play. Aeschylus had no knowledge of the Persian Court and no conception of how Xerxes' expedition and the defeat of Salamis might appear to the Persian nobility or royal family. The characters all talk Greek and, on occasion, refer to themselves as barbarians. As evidence for specifically Persian history the play is valueless. The messenger, however, in bringing news of the disaster gives a detailed description of the battle which, considering that Aeschylus wrote for an audience which must have contained many eyewitnesses, is of much historical significance. It was written in dignified verse by a great poet. What follows is plain prose and gives the sense but none of the poetry.

The messenger is speaking to Xerxes' mother, Atossa.

A Greek from the Athenian host came to tell your son Xerxes that when night came the Greeks would stay no longer, but, leaping to their oars, would flee for their lives, helter skelter, under cover of the dark. Xerxes, blind to the treachery of the Greek, and to the spite of the gods, on hearing this at once gave orders to all his captains that as soon as the burning rays of the sun left the earth, and darkness took his place in the precinct of the sky, they were to dispose the massed ranks of their ships in three files and guard the foaming seaways that gave egress from the bay, while other ships were to encircle the island of Ajax [i.e. Salamis which, in Homer, was the home of the hero Ajax]. Should the Greeks escape their evil destiny by finding some secret passage, every Persian captain would be decapitated. So much he told them in sanguine mood, not knowing what the gods had in store. And they obediently took food, and each oarsman carefully set his oar in place. When the sun's brightness was dimmed and night came on, each oarsman and each marine went to his ship. The lines of warships urged one another on, and so they made their way, each in his appointed station. All night the admirals kept them on patrol. The night wore on and yet nowhere did the Greek fleet seek stealthily to break out. When dawn, with her white horses, shed bright light on all the land, there first came from the Greeks the sound of a triumphant song, echoed back from the island's rocks, and fear fell on all the barbarians, thus finding themselves deceived in their hopes. Not in flight were the Greeks singing their hymn of triumph, but surging forward to battle with bold confidence, while a trumpet's blare fired their souls, and in unison their oars struck the foam. Quickly they all came in sight. First the right wing led the ordered lines; then the whole fleet came out and a great shout was heard. 'Sons of the Greeks, go, bring freedom to your native land, to your children, your wives, to the shrines of your ancestral gods and the tombs of your forefathers. All is now at stake.' And then from our ships there was an answering shout in the Persian tongue, and this was no time to hang back. At once ship struck ship with bronze-sheathed beak. A Greek ship struck first and sheared off the whole stern-post of a Phoenician. Others then aimed their ships at other ships.

At first the mass of the Persian fleet held its own, but such was the crush in the narrow space that no ship could help another. Instead they fouled each other with their brazen beaks and smashed their rows of oars. Skilfully the Greeks struck from all sides and capsized the Persian ships. No longer was the sea visible, so full was it of wrecks and slaughtered men. The shores and reefs were covered with corpses as every surviving Persian ship rowed off in disorderly flight, while the Greeks with splintered oars, or stumps of wreckage, struck and hewed at the Persian sailors as if they were a catch of tunny fish. Until dark night stopped the slaughter, shrieks and wailings resounded over all the sea. Not in ten days could I complete the tale, were I to tell it all in proper order. Never did such a multitude of men perish in one day.

(AESCHYLUS, *The Persians*, ll. 354-432)

But that, says the messenger, is not all. There is worse to come. 'What could be worse than what you have told?' asks Atossa. 'The flower of the Persian army, strong, brave, well-born and outstanding in their loyalty, met a shameful and ignominious death.' 'How did they die?' asks Atossa.

> Off Salamis [answers the messenger], there is a small island, inhospitable to ships but whose shores are haunted by the dance-loving god Pan.
>
> (*The Persians*, ll. 447-9)

So he tells of the massacre of the Persian troops whom Xerxes had landed on Psyttaleia. After witnessing this, he says, Xerxes tore his robes and ordered the army to begin a headlong retreat, during which it suffered many hardships.

The ghost

After many lamentations by the Chorus, Atossa returns from the palace, where she had gone to put on mourning clothes. With offerings of milk and wine and olive oil and flowers and with prayers, Atossa and the Chorus summon from his grave the recently dead Darius, whose wisdom is contrasted with the boastful folly of Xerxes. On being informed of the disaster of Salamis, he attributes it to Xerxes' arrogance in flogging the Hellespont, and to the gods who grudge too much prosperity to mortals. He warns against any further attempt to conquer Greece, while prophesying that there will yet be a disastrous battle at Plataea.

Hard facts

As always these are not easy to come by. Herodotus' account of the battle agrees in essentials with that of Aeschylus, as one would expect it to, since Herodotus must have been familiar with *The Persians*. It includes more detail – names of captains on both sides, several anecdotes (not all relevant), two prophecies which came true and two stories of supernatural intervention which he does not guarantee to be genuine. Where the accounts differ is over the aftermath. According to Herodotus, Xerxes delayed several days before deciding to evacuate Attica and return to Sardis, during which time the Greek fleet remained in readiness expecting another attack. The precipitate flight described by the messenger in *The Persians* can be ascribed to poetic licence, as Aeschylus needs to get Xerxes back to

Susa soon after his messenger if he is to make an appearance in the play.

Despite the brilliant success of the Greek fleet, the war was far from won. The Persians had suffered severe losses, especially from among the crack Phoenician crews, and many of the Persian, Indian and Scythian marines had been drowned, since they did not know how to swim to safety as the Greeks did. Even so the Persian fleet still outnumbered the Greek fleet, while the Persian army, having crushed the defenders of Thermopylae, could still regard itself as invincible. Nevertheless the end of the campaigning season was approaching and Xerxes may well have felt that it was neither necessary nor desirable to prolong his absence from the administrative centres of his empire. His general (and son-in-law) Mardonius was a very capable and experienced commander and should have – so it must have seemed – no difficulty in completing, by a combination of diplomatic and military measures, the purposes of the invasion.

So Xerxes ordered his fleet to sail to the Hellespont to protect the bridge of boats, and led his army back to Thessaly. Here he left Mardonius with some 100,000 picked troops, and returned to Sardis – but without the sacred chariot of Ahura-Mazda. It had been stolen by the Thracians.

The winter and spring of 480-479

After the Persians had retreated, the Athenians returned to Athens. Mardonius spent the winter with his army in northern Greece. His second-in-command, Artabazus, stopped off on his way back from escorting Xerxes to the Hellespont to besiege two cities on the isthmus of Pallene. One of the cities had revolted and the other, he suspected, might do so. The city that had revolted successfully defied him for three months. The one that was merely suspected he captured, slaughtering all the inhabitants. He finally abandoned the siege of the other city and left the area to join Mardonius, but not before he lost many of his troops from drowning. Tempted by a peculiarly low tide to send troops across the exposed shore in the hope of taking the defences in the rear, he lost them all when a returning flood-tide caught them before they had reached dry land.

Meanwhile Mardonius sent King Alexander of Macedon to the Athenians with a message tempting them to desert their allies. If they did they were promised forgiveness, liberty to live by their own laws, an addition of territory and the rebuilding of all their temples. The

Spartans sent a counter-embassy urging the Athenians to reject Mardonius' terms.

To Alexander the Athenians replied that he was to report to Mardonius as follows:

> The Athenians say that as long as the sun travels on his usual course they will never make terms with Xerxes, but will continue to defend themselves, trusting in the help of their gods and heroes, whom he has insulted by burning their temples and their statues.

To the Spartans the Athenians said:

> We will never make peace with Xerxes. Therefore send out an army as quickly as you can, for we think it will not be long before the enemy invades our country again. He will march as soon as he hears that we have rejected his proposals; so now, before he reaches Attica, is the time for you to meet him in Boeotia.
>
> (HERODOTUS, 8.144)

However the Spartans would not move from southern Greece until they had completed the wall across the Isthmus. They also (according to Herodotus) had their minds on a religious festival they were celebrating. So the Athenians had to evacuate Attica again and move everything they could to safety in the island of Salamis. They sent an angry embassy to Sparta. The Spartans kept the ambassadors waiting for a reply, until at last they informed them that their army had quietly marched out the night before and was already on its way north.

Mardonius withdrew from Attica to Boeotia, ravaging as he went. In Boeotia the terrain was more suited to the Persian cavalry, and in Boeotia he had a base in the city of Thebes, which had medised. The Spartan general Pausanias, who was acting as regent for his nephew (the young son of Leonidas) commanded the allied army. He followed Mardonius into Boeotia, staying on the rough broken ground in the foothills of Mount Cithaeron, where the Persian cavalry could not operate. He had nearly 40,000 heavy-armed, and about 70,000 light-armed infantry but no cavalry. Against these Mardonius had a force of some 300,000 men, consisting of Persian heavy-armed cavalry and infantry, together with light-armed cavalry from medising Greek states and various provinces of the Persian Empire.

What precisely were the manoeuvres that led up to the Battle of Plataea has always been a matter of controversy for scholars, but the course of the battle itself seems clear.

The Greeks, on Pausanias' orders, carried out a tactical withdrawal from the positions they had taken up. Mardonius (possibly misinterpreting this as a confused retreat) advanced to attack the Spartan contingent and halted his troops who formed a barricade of their wicker shields. From behind these they showered the Spartans with arrows. Pausanias kept his men standing firm until the Persian ranks had become too tightly packed to manoeuvre. Then he ordered them to charge. The longer Spartan spears and their heavier armour put the Persians at a grave disadvantage. They fought bravely, but when Mardonius was killed they broke, and fled to a stockade previously constructed in their rear. The other Greek troops came up, notably the Athenians, and forced their way into the stockade and slaughtered them all. The bulk of the Persian army had been destroyed for the loss of some 160 Greek lives. Mardonius' second-in-command, who had remained in reserve, marched away without stopping until he had crossed the Hellespont.

On the same day the Greek fleet put ashore at Mykale in Ionia and annihilated a Persian force of some 40,000 men.

Not only was Xerxes' threat to Greece removed but the Greeks had carried the war into the Persian Empire.

Chapter 7
Aftermath of the Invasion

Some anticlimaxes: Greece

Within ten years of the Battle of Plataea the two leaders who had done most towards achieving victory were both disgraced: the Spartan Pausanias put to death; the Athenian Themistocles in exile, soon to have a price on his head. The Spartan admiral Leotykhidas who had commanded the sea and land forces at the battle of Mykale, was also in exile. The rigorous Spartan education, so effective in producing tough soldiers who would die before disobeying orders, did not prepare them for exercising authority over other Greeks. They quickly made themselves unpopular and were very apt to be corrupted by Persian gold and the sight of Persian luxury. Themistocles was a victim of Athenian democratic politics and had been merely ostracised, but while living in exile he was implicated in some very suspicious correspondence between Pausanias and Xerxes and had to flee. He escaped to Persia where he was welcomed, either because it was believed by the Persians that he had genuinely tried to betray the Greeks at Salamis and after, or simply because the Persian kings always liked to have Greek defectors at hand as sources of information and advice.

The Athenian alliance

The Ionian Greeks – who had been liberated by the battle of Mykale – found the Spartans so officious and arrogant that they preferred to be led by the Athenians. The Athenian fleet was commanded at this time by Aristides who had a well-deserved reputation for fairness. On behalf of the Athenians he arranged a defensive and offensive alliance between Athens and the Ionian cities. Some twelve years after the battle of Mykale the fleet of the Athenian alliance under the command of Kimon, the son of Miltiades (the general who had commanded the Athenians at Marathon) fought a combined sea and land battle at the mouth of the Eurymedon river, on the southern coast of Asia Minor. The Persian forces were gathering to reconquer the Ionian cities, but

61

Kimon attacked before their fleet was fully assembled and annihilated both fleet and army.

Rivalries

The uneasy alliance between Athens and Sparta which had defeated the Persian invasion lasted for another seventeen years, but it was under increasing strain. The victories of Marathon, Salamis, Mykale and the Eurymedon had made Athens self-confident and ambitious; the liberation of Aegean trade from Persians and pirates helped to make her prosperous; and her alliance with the Ionian cities and the islands gave her command of a navy which was supreme in the eastern Mediterranean. Gradually she transformed her alliance into an empire, from which the member cities were not permitted to withdraw. If they did they were attacked and punished. On the other hand they were encouraged to exchange the obligation to supply ships to the alliance's navy for an obligation to pay tribute. After the Aegean waters had been made safe from the Persian navy, the Athenians felt entitled to use surplus tribute money to rebuild the temples of Athens which had been destroyed by Xerxes.

Democrats and aristocrats and the Peloponnesian War

At the same time the Athenians were making their constitution more and more democratic. Paradoxically the leader of the democratic party was an aristocrat, Pericles the son of that Xanthippos whose dog had swum all the way to Salamis. The effect of these changes was to polarise the Greek world. Aristocrats everywhere admired Sparta and, when practicable, looked to her for support against the democrats in their cities; while the democrats looked to Athens. The final outcome of Athenian ambitions and the hostility and resentment it aroused was the so-called Peloponnesian War, between Sparta and her allies on the one hand and Athens and her subjects on the other. It began in 431 BC, 48 years after the battles of Plataea and Mykale, and lasted twenty-seven years, with a truce of five years in the middle. It was made more bloodthirsty in several of the cities taking part by coups and countercoups in which democrats massacred aristocrats or aristocrats massacred democrats, depending on which was on top. As the war went on it became more and more bitter and atrocities were increasingly committed by both sides, particularly by the Athenians. In the first years Athens had been devastated by a plague which killed about one third of the population. According to the Athenian historian Thucydides, its effect was to introduce a spirit of recklessness and cynicism into Athenian society, since the plague struck down indiscriminately the honourable and the lawless, those who dutifully worshipped the gods and those who did not. While sudden death was an ever-present threat, fear of either punishment or disgrace lost all power to restrain men from pursuing the pleasure of the moment, and few gave any thought for the consequences of their actions.

In 415 BC, some ten years after the plague had departed as abruptly as it had come, the Athenians mounted an overambitious expedition to conquer Sicily. It ended in disaster and cost them 200 ships (and their crews) and 4,000 cavalry and infantry. From then on they were on the defensive, but they still refused several opportunities to make peace. In 404 BC the war ended suddenly with a disaster to the Athenians' last fleet which left them with no alternative to unconditional surrender.

Some anticlimaxes: Persia

For the seventy-five years which saw Athens rise to imperial greatness and finally plunge to disaster, the history of the Persian Empire remains obscure. Herodotus, who was an artist, a moralist and a story-teller as well as an historian, ends his history of the great invasion with two stories, one probably fictitious, the other probably true in outline, if not in detail. The fictitious story tells of some Persians who went to Cyrus, after he had conquered Media, and asked him why he did not lead his people down from the harsh plateau where they were born, to live in comfort in some part of the fruitful lowlands. To this Cyrus replied that if he did so they must be prepared no longer to rule, but to be ruled, because it was not in the nature of any land to produce both bountiful fruit and warlike men: soft climates, he said breed soft men.

Xerxes' intrigue

The other story concerns Xerxes. While he was at Sardis after the final defeat of his expedition he fell in love with the wife of his brother Masistes. Masistes was governor of Bactria but had been with the army at the battle of Mykale, and came to Sardis with his wife after that battle. When Xerxes failed to seduce his sister-in-law through amorous messages he thought he might have more success if her daughter Artaynte were married to his son Darius. So he arranged this. He then returned to Susa, where his new daughter-in-law came to live in his palace. Soon he found that he had fallen in love with her and no longer loved her mother. With the daughter – his daughter-in-law and also his niece – he was more successful, and for a time succeeded in keeping their love affair secret.

A doomed family

The climax of the story turns on the Persian tradition that the Great King might never unsay any promise he had made, and that at his birthday feast he might deny to no one any gift he or she asked for. At the centre of the tragedy is a very beautiful robe woven for Xerxes by his wife Amestris. This robe he wore when he visited his daughter-in-law Artaynte. Overcome by passionate gratitude he told her to ask for whatever she wanted and promised it should be hers.

> Because fate had ordained that she should bring ruin on herself and all her family, she said to Xerxes, 'Will you give me whatever I ask for?' Xerxes promised on oath, thinking she would ask for anything but the robe, yet that is exactly what she demanded as soon as he had given his promise. Xerxes did everything he could to avoid giving it, for no other reason than that he was afraid of Amestris. He guessed that she was already suspicious and would take this as proof of what he was up to. He offered cities to Artaynte and unlimited gold and an army for her to command personally (a typically Persian gift), but all was in vain. So Artaynte got the robe, was delighted with her present, wore it and flaunted it.
>
> (HERODOTUS, 9.109)

The rest of the story can be guessed – or read in Book 9 of Herodotus' *Histories* (109-13).

The significance of both stories lies in the depiction of the Persian Empire as the achievement of a great and good man – Cyrus – consolidated by another great and good man – Darius – which came to disaster and decline when inherited by a vain and arrogant but weak-willed successor. This picture, already implicit in Aeschylus' *The Persians*, was extended into later reigns by subsequent Greek writers and appears in references to the Persian Empire in the Old Testament (Deutero-Isaiah, Ezra and Esther). Since there were no histories written by Persians to counterbalance this picture, it has become a cliché of European literature – the oriental despotism doomed to degenerate into the rule of weak and debauched despots dominated by imperious queens or crafty eunuchs, and weakened by female rivalries and harem conspiracies. Racine's *Bajazet* – especially in his preface – and Shelley's *Hellas*, both written with an eye on *The Persians*, transfer the cliché to their representation of the Ottoman court in their own centuries. As regards the later reigns of the Achaemenid monarchy the picture went virtually unchallenged until quite recently, when scholars began to consider evidence from Babylonian chronicles and negative evidence from Persian excavations. From these it began to look as if the traditional picture mirrored not so much the realities of the Persian Court and Persian government as a tendency of Greek writers to see in Persia, which they neither knew nor understood, the antithesis of democratic Greek ideals. It can also be seen as having served to flatter the hopes of some Greeks that if the Greek states would only compose their internecine quarrels they would have little difficulty in toppling a decadent and incompetent Persian monarchy.

The end of Xerxes and the reign of Artaxerxes

Some fourteen years after the invasion of Greece the commander of the royal guard conspired with the eunuch in charge of the royal bedchamber to assassinate Xerxes and put the blame on Xerxes' eldest son Darius, who was promptly killed by Xerxes' second son Artaxerxes. The commander of the royal guard then tried to assassinate Artaxerxes also, but failed and was killed himself. The third of Xerxes' sons was away governing Bactria and had to be defeated before Artaxerxes was secure on his throne. During his reign, which lasted 43 years, Egypt revolted, but was eventually reconquered by one of his generals, despite the intervention of an Athenian fleet. The Athenian fleet met with disaster, but two years later another Athenian fleet won a victory over the Persians' fleet off Cyprus. After this, Athens and King Artaxerxes made peace. The terms were that the Persians would leave the Ionian Greeks alone and the Greeks would not interfere in the affairs of the Persian Empire.

Persian gold and the Peloponnesian War

Artaxerxes died seven years after the Greeks had begun their

Peloponnesian War. He had only one legitimate son, named Xerxes. After this Xerxes had reigned only 45 days he was murdered by a half-brother (a son of Artaxerxes and a Babylonian concubine). The half-brother (his name was Sogdianos) reigned for six months before he was overthrown by another half-brother, who was also the son of Artaxerxes by a Babylonian concubine. This half-brother became king as Darius II and reigned for 18 years. He was married to a half-sister, by name Parysatis, a daughter of Artaxerxes by yet another of his concubines.

During the reign of Darius II the Persians discovered that, because of the Peloponnesian War, they could do more harm to the Greeks by the use of their gold than Darius or Xerxes had done by invasion. For most of the time they supported the Spartans by paying their soldiers and sailors, but from time to time they changed sides and gave subsidies to the Athenians. This policy was carried out by the Persian governors of the provinces in western Asia Minor who often acted in rivalry with one another. For this reason Darius sent his younger son Cyrus to take charge of all Persian affairs in western Asia Minor. Cyrus had private reasons for wanting the Spartans to be quickly victorious, so he ended the policy of letting the two sides weaken each other and supplied the help that enabled the Spartans to defeat the Athenian fleet and end the war.

The fifth century – a review

(a) Before the invasion: Greece
When the century opened there were, as always, Greek cities fighting one another; principally Athens fighting to conquer her trade rival and near neighbour, the island and city of Aegina. Quite recently Athens had got rid of her tyrants who had begun well by beautifying Athens and making her strong, but ended badly with harshness and executions. After their expulsion Athens had taken the first steps towards the total democracy that was in power during most of the Peloponnesian War.

Sparta had built herself a strong and lasting military alliance with all the states of southern Greece except for the state of Argos, which had always been her rival and enemy. However Sparta had recently crushed Argos in a battle in which Argos had lost so many of her heavy-armed infantrymen that she was incapable of making war for a whole generation. Sparta had a very simple foreign policy. It consisted of hostility to tyrants, to democracies and to Persia. She had helped the Athenians to get rid of their tyrants and then tried unsuccessfully to intervene against the budding democracy. Her army was at the peak of its efficiency and regarded by other Greeks as nearly invincible.

(b) Before the invasion: Persia

At the beginning of the fifth century Persia had in fifty years become by far the largest empire the world had yet known. Xerxes' father Darius had welded it into an efficiently administered organisation by making use of the bureaucratic systems and personnel of the empires his predecessors had conquered. Within the Empire peace was kept, trade flourished and a not too burdensome tribute was imposed and collected without corruption or injustice.

(c) After the invasion: Greece

Only in patriotic solidarity between Greek states (panhellenism) was the rest of the century an anticlimax. Defeat of the Persians was a brief interlude in the sad story of Greek cities fighting one another in the pursuit by the stronger of power and glory, and by the weaker of independence and security.

There were massacres and enslavement of Greeks by Greeks both before the Persian Wars and after.

On the other hand the fifth century was – particularly at Athens – the great age of artistic, literary and intellectual achievement, concentrated, as never before or since, into the short span of seventy years or so.

(d) After the invasion: Persia

During the period between the Persian Wars and the last fifteen years of the fifth century the Greeks had only peripheral contacts with the Persian Empire and therefore no particular incentive to interest themselves in Persian history. After this date the Athenians and Spartans were in rivalry, firstly for Persian financial support and later, after the Athenian defeat, in campaigns fought in Asia Minor, the Levant and Egypt in which the Spartans fought against the Persians, and Athenian commanders of mercenary forces fought for them. Both the financial transactions and the military operations brought the Greeks into contact with Persian noblemen governing the provinces bordering on Ionia. Consequently there is very little Greek evidence for the history of Persia between around 470 and 415, and after that date the Greek information is mainly about the careers and personalities of the various Persian governors with whom the Greeks dealt, or about court life in narratives derived from Ktesias and Dinon. What was happening in all but the westernmost districts of the Empire is virtually unknown.

To this there is one exception: the building programme of the Persian kings. Here the evidence is concrete, and available to the archaeologist. Darius had begun building for himself the palace of Persopolis: Xerxes enlarged, embellished and extended it. It was a joint achievement which embodied the greatness of the Empire, blending Egyptian, Assyrian, Babylonian and Greek artistic traditions, and it was constructed by assembling craftsmen from wherever the best were to be found within, and even beyond, the extensive frontiers of the Empire. If the palace buildings of Persepolis had survived in as good a state of preservation as the Parthenon, they would have made a significant and not unworthy subject for comparison and contrast. Building of great splendour was continued by the later Achaemenid kings on the site of Persepolis and elsewhere.

Chapter 8
The Ten Thousand

Cyrus and Artaxerxes

Darius II died just as the Peloponnesian War ended. He was succeeded by the elder of his two sons who became king as Artaxerxes II. This was despite the efforts of Darius' queen Parysatis who wanted her favourite son Cyrus to be king. The two brothers hated one another and Cyrus, even before the end of the Peloponnesian War, was planning to supplant his brother.

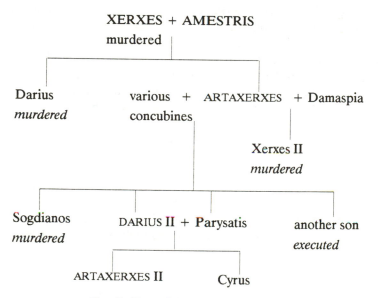

Family Tree of Cyrus and Artaxerxes

Cyrus' ambitions

Cyrus had a princely manner and was generous, courageous, imaginative and good at winning the loyalty of those who served him. Persian tradition, however, gave to the Great King the choice of his successor, and Darius had chosen Artaxerxes. Cyrus' ambitions were well known and before his father's death he had been in trouble for murdering two cousins who failed to show him due deference. If he had been kept at court he would probably not have survived long, but Parysatis, though she had not been able to make him king, had been able to persuade Artaxerxes to send him back to govern the western-most provinces of the Empire. There, Artaxerxes may have thought, he would be too busy dealing with troublesome Greeks and too far from the court to hatch any plots.

Cyrus' problems

To set out from Ionia to supplant the Great King in Susa was a very bold, if not rash, undertaking. Cyrus' great-great-grandfather, Darius, had seized the throne from a reigning king, but then he had the support of six other leading Persian nobles and had control of the crack Persian troops which he had been commanding in the Egyptian campaign of Cambyses – and, even so, he had a year of hard fighting before he was securely on the throne. Cyrus' father and mother had supplanted their half-brother Sogdianos, but he had already antagonised the royal troops by killing their commander; besides, Darius and Parysatis had started from Hyrcania, where Darius was governor, near to the heart of the Empire. Ionia was 2,000 miles from Susa over some very difficult country. Long before Cyrus could lead any troops to the heart of the empire, Artaxerxes would have been warned and given time to assemble the flower of the Persian army – especially as a personal enemy of Cyrus (his name was Tissaphernes) was governor of the neighbouring province where he could keep an eye on him. Besides, apart from 300 Greek mercenaries who formed his bodyguard, his only troops were those supplied to him for fighting against rebellious mountain tribesmen.

Cyrus' plans

Cyrus however, from what he had witnessed at the end of the Peloponnesian War, seems to have formed a shrewd estimate of the relative value of the Greek and Persian infantry of his day. Since long before the fifth century there had been Greeks who hired themselves out to Middle Eastern monarchs as mercenary soldiers, and, during the fifth century, Greeks had been paid by Persian kings to fight against rebellious Egyptian pharoahs, and by rebellious Egyptian pharoahs to fight against Persian kings. Cyrus knew that once the Peloponnesian War was over there would be no shortage of hardened soldiers who preferred military to civilian employment; and so it was.

Cyrus, while he had been backing the Spartans against the Athenians, had been in contact with many Greek officers. He quietly let it be known to several of these that he needed about ten thousand heavy-armed Greek infantry to help him to subdue some rebellious tribes who lived in a mountainous region of his province, or else to help him in his personal operations against Tissaphernes.

The most experienced of his Greek officers was a Spartan, Klearkhos, who had held several important commands during and after the war but had been exiled by the Spartan government for disobeying orders. The most important of Cyrus' Greeks for posterity was an Athenian, Xenophon, who had gained some experience of war as a cavalryman in the last years before Athens' defeat, and wanted more. So he joined Cyrus' mercenaries in an amateur capacity, simply as the friend of one of the commanders. His importance to posterity is that years after the expedition he wrote an account of it, probably in order to correct what he considered to be errors in an account written by another of the leaders of the Ten Thousand. That account has been lost, so scholars can only make intelligent guesses as to whether Xenophon told untruths, remembered things wrongly or exaggerated his own part in the later stages of the adventure.

The expedition sets out

Cyrus assembled his Asiatic troops and most of his mercenaries at Sardis early in 401 BC, announcing that he was off to deal with rebellious Pisidians. Tissaphernes, however, was not fooled and rode at once to Susa to warn Artaxerxes. On his way to Pisidia Cyrus was joined by the rest of his mercenaries. After fourteen days of marching, and another eleven days to rest and review his troops, Cyrus came to the province of Cilicia, where the hereditary ruler (his title was Syennesis) was faced with a dilemma. His province included a narrow pass through which Cyrus' army must pass. Artaxerxes would expect him to defend this pass. If he failed to do so and Artaxerxes won, he could expect a very unpleasant end. So he cleverly hedged his bets and let Cyrus through with a pretence at resistance, while sending one of his sons to Artaxerxes with professions of loyalty, and his wife to Cyrus with money to pay his troops.

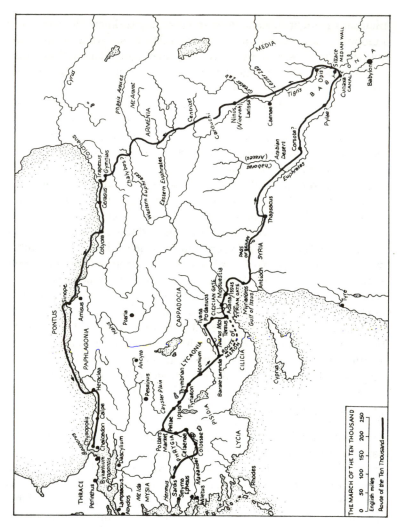

Fig. 11. To Babylonia and back.

Mutiny

It took the army thirteen days of marching through Cilicia to reach its capital, Tarsus. There the Greek troops halted and refused to go any further. The pretext of subduing the Pisidians had lost all credibility. Klearkhos, who probably alone of the officers knew Cyrus' true destination, made two cunning speeches, pretending to be anxious to do whatever the troops wanted. In this way he tricked them into agreeing to march for another twelve days. Cyrus was now telling them that he wanted to attack another personal enemy, Abrocomas, the governor of Syria, who would probably flee. To clinch the argument they were promised a fifty per-cent pay rise.

After twelve days they were joined by another Spartan general and 700 troops who had come by sea, and by 400 mercenaries who had just deserted Abrocomas. Twelve days more marching brought them to the Euphrates River. There Cyrus told the Greeks his real plans. They grumbled, but it was too late to go back, so they crossed the river and marched on.

The desert

The march down the Euphrates took them through the edge of the Syrian desert (they called it Arabia). They saw no trees, only aromatic shrubs. They did see many wild animals: gazelles, wild asses, ostriches and bustards, but the wild asses and the ostriches ran faster than their horses. They found, however, that they could catch the wild asses by hunting them in relays. Ass flesh tasted delicious, like red deer only more tender. They never caught an ostrich.

Still marching along the Euphrates they came to a city where they rested and collected provisions. Then for thirteen days they marched through empty desert. Many of the baggage animals died for want of fodder and the Greek soldiers had to eat nothing but meat, which did not suit them since they were used to a vegetarian diet.

The battle of Kounaxa

Finally their march down the left bank of the Euphrates brought them out of the desert into Babylonia.

Sixty miles from Babylon the armies of Cyrus and Artaxerxes met.

The battle was described by Xenophon, by Plutarch in a biography he wrote of Artaxerxes, and by Diodorus the Sicilian. No modern scholar can make any military sense of the accounts (which all differ). However three episodes seem indisputable. The Greeks under the command of Klearkhos with their right flank protected by the Euphrates, charged and routed the left wing of Artaxerxes' army with little or no cost to themselves. Meanwhile in the centre of the battlefield Cyrus led a wild cavalry charge and attempted to kill his brother with his own hand. He wounded him and knocked him off his horse but was himself killed in the scrimmage. All Cyrus' Asiatic troops, the moment they learnt their leader was dead, knew that there was nothing left for them to fight for; so they fled.

Two dilemmas

The Greeks assumed that they had won Cyrus' battle for him since it was not until the next day that they discovered he was dead. Messengers arrived to say that Artaxerxes had won the battle and the Greeks must hand over their arms and be grateful for any mercy that Artaxerxes might show them. The more spirited of the Greek generals asked in reply, 'If Artaxerxes had won the battle, why did he have to request their arms instead of just coming to take them?'

Still, the Greeks were in a jam. They could, it seemed, defeat Artaxerxes' armies – at least for the moment – but they needed help from the Persians to find food for themselves and for their pack animals. Besides, there were no maps, so how could they find their way back to friendly territory? They could not go back the way they had come because, without Cyrus to supply provisions, they could never survive the crossing of the Syrian desert, nor could they recross the Euphrates if the army of Artaxerxes was there to stop them.

Artaxerxes, too, was in a jam. He had some 10,000 Greek soldiers in the middle of his Empire. If he attacked them, at worst his troops would be routed again, at best he might fight the Greeks to a standstill at the cost of some of his best troops. If he left them alone they would march about plundering his lands. If they got back safely to Greece all Greeks would think that the rich Persian Empire could not defend itself against a Greek army.

Klearkhos' leadership

Now that Cyrus was dead the Greeks did not have anyone to tell them when and where to march. They made a solemn pact with Ariaios, the commander of Cyrus' Persian troops, not to betray one another, but they did not trust him. So, without actually electing Klearkhos as their general they simply accepted his leadership, since he was by far the most experienced of their generals.

Klearkhos was a tough character, about fifty years old, who lived for soldiering. He enjoyed hardship and danger, he was cool in any crisis and he was experienced in all the tricks and stratagems of campaigning. He was very strict, gave many harsh punishments and believed that a soldier should be more frightened of his commander than of the enemy. His soldiers hated him when things were going well, but when they were in danger they were happy to be commanded by someone so strict, so experienced, so self-confident and so determined.

For several weeks there was a battle of wits between the Persians and Klearkhos. The Persian commanders watched the Greeks from a distance, persuaded Cyrus' Persian troops to desert them, sent confusing messages and, from time to time, rode up with offers of a truce. They promised guides to take the Greeks where they could buy provisions, and they even promised friendship. They behaved like a cat with a mouse, except that they were very wary of the mouse. Klearkhos took every opportunity to play upon their wariness by showing off the size, good discipline and superior arms of the Greek army. He never let the Persians guess what he was going to do. He accepted the truce, but kept his troops ready to fight. Under truce both armies marched southwards and then eastwards towards the Tigris river. Here is Xenophon's account:

> The Persians led the way but Klearkhos, in spite of the truce, kept the army in battle order. He himself commanded the rearguard. They kept coming to ditches and canals full of water. These could not be crossed without bridges. So they built bridges of palm trunks, both of trees that had fallen and of trees that they cut down themselves. Here you could see what a good commander Klearkhos was. He held his spear in his left hand and a stick in his right. If he thought anyone of the bridge-builders was shirking, he picked him out and beat him. At the same time he waded into the mud and helped with the work, shaming everyone into working as hard as he did. The men under thirty had been selected for the bridge-building, but even the older men joined in when they saw Klearkhos being so energetic.
>
> The reason that Klearkhos was hurrying on the work was that he was suspicious about the amount of water in the ditches. It was not the season for irrigating the plain and he suspected that Artaxerxes had let the water in on purpose to make the journey seem all the more difficult and dangerous to the Greeks.
>
> (XENOPHON, *Anabasis*, 2.3)

A friend for the Greeks?

Artaxerxes went off to Babylon to get his wound healed (by Ktesias, or so Ktesias claimed) and Tissaphernes rode up to the Greeks and asked to speak to the generals. Through an interpreter he told them that, as governor of the westernmost provinces, he was a neighbour of the Greeks, and therefore wanted to be friends with them. He had asked Artaxerxes, he said, for permission to rescue them and escort them back to Ionia. Artaxerxes had granted this wish, according to Tissaphernes, because of his gratitude to him for his help in defeating and killing Cyrus.

Fig. 12. Tissaphernes portrayed on a coin dated ca. 400 BC.

So Tissaphernes and the Greek generals swore oaths. Tissaphernes swore that he would lead the Greeks without treachery. The Greek generals swore that they would march through the country without doing any harm. Tissaphernes then kept them waiting for twenty days. After this he returned with the troops he was taking to his province. With him was another Persian grandee, who had just married Artaxerxes' daughter and was on his way to be governor of Eastern Armenia.

Both armies set off, at first marching south-east until they had crossed the Tigris river by a bridge of boats. Then they turned northwards, keeping the Tigris on their left hand. The two armies watched one another suspiciously and were careful to bivouac at a good distance from one another. In this manner they covered some 250 miles. On their way they had met with a half-brother of Cyrus and Artaxerxes who was bringing an army, belatedly, to support

Artaxerxes. He halted to take a look at the Greeks, so Klearkhos led them past, strung out two by two and halting from time to time, so as to give the impression of a very large army. When they reached the confluence of the River Zab with the Tigris they halted for three days, and there Klearkhos came to believe he could trust Tissaphernes. He asked for an interview and tried to strike a bargain. He offered to lead the Greek mercenaries on any campaign that Tissaphernes wanted to undertake: in return, Tissaphernes must treat him as a friend, just as Cyrus had done. This was Klearkhos' first and fatal mistake. It was caused by the inability of almost any Greek to comprehend the nature of the Persian monarchy. This inability had led Klearkhos, when he learnt of Cyrus' death, to turn to Ariaios and offer to make him king, not appreciating that only a member of the royal family would be acceptable to the Persians and that Ariaios' only hope of survival was to make his peace with Artaxerxes as quickly as possible and hope that the influence of Cyrus' mother, Parysatis, might win him a pardon. The Greeks could not be expected to realise that a power struggle was going on at court betweeen Parysatis and Artaxerxes' wife Statira (who may or may not have been Tissaphernes' sister). Tissaphernes had been given the job of getting rid of the Greeks. Any failure to do so would have played into the hands of Parysatis, who hated him for his part in the death of her favourite son. The Greeks may have guessed that they were being used to pay off personal scores when they were led by Tissaphernes to some villages belonging to Parysatis and told that they might plunder them at will. However this was not enough to disabuse Klearkhos of the idea that he could be on the same terms with Tissaphernes as he had been with Cyrus.

Treachery

Tissaphernes pretended to be delighted at Klearkhos' proposal. He entertained Klearkhos to dinner and invited him to bring all the other generals and captains to a meeting next day. He said that some of these had secretly informed him that Klearkhos was planning to attack him, an accusation that Klearkhos was more ready to believe because he suspected that one of the other Greek generals was trying to get command of the 10,000 mercenaries. (This general was the Thessalian Meno, whom Xenophon disliked but who is sympathetically portrayed by Plato in the Dialogue of that name.)

Klearkhos spent that night as Tissaphernes' guest and next day went back to the Greek camp and persuaded four generals and twenty captains to go with him to Tissaphernes. About 200 other soldiers went with them to buy provisions in the Persian camp.

> When they came to the entrance of Tissaphernes' tent the generals were invited inside...while the captains waited outside. Quite soon afterwards a signal was given and at the same moment those inside the tent were seized and those outside were cut down. Then some Persian horsemen rode over the plain killing all the Greeks they came across, including the slaves.
>
> The Greeks who had remained in the camp were amazed to see all this activity and could not make out what was going on until an Arcadian named Nikarkhos arrived with a wound in his belly, holding his guts in his hand. From him they learned all that had happened.
>
> (XENOPHON, *Anabasis*, 2.5)

Chapter 9
The Ten Thousand on Their Own

Another invitation to surrender

When the Greeks heard what Nikarkhos had to tell, they rushed in panic to pick up their arms, expecting an attack at any moment.

There was no attack, but, instead, Ariaios and two other noblemen who had been particularly loyal friends of Cyrus rode up with 300 armed horsemen. They asked any officer present to come forward to hear what the Great King had to say to them. Two of the Greeks' remaining generals went forward with an armed escort and were joined by Xenophon, who was anxious to know what had happened to his friend Proxenos. (Proxenos had gone to the conference with Klearkhos.) To these three Ariaios told a tale of Klearkhos breaking his oath and plotting against Tissaphernes. He had got what he deserved, he said, and was dead. Two of the other generals had denounced him and were being honoured for it. 'The Great King demands your arms,' he continued, 'for he says they belong to him by right since they formerly belonged to his slave Cyrus.'

The Greeks were not deceived by this tale and one of the officers roundly abused the three Persians for their treachery. Xenophon, more subtle, said that if their tale was true, then they should send back to them the two 'honoured' generals. They, being friends to both sides, would give everyone the best advice. This led to a lengthy discussion among the Persians, after which they rode away without replying.

An election and an assembly

The Greeks had now lost their leaders and knew that the Persians were determined to destroy them. They were in despair and could neither eat nor sleep, thinking they would never see their homes and families again. Xenophon, however, did at last doze off and had a dream, sent, he believed, as a message from heaven. Though the dream showed him his father's house struck by lightning and in flames, he interpreted it, since lightning comes from Zeus, as a message of hope. It set him thinking that if the Persians were going to attack them in the morning, he and the other Greeks should be making preparations to defend themselves. So he called together all the surviving captains of the contingent which his lost friend, Proxenos, had commanded. When they were assembled he made a stirring speech, pointing out the horrible fate that awaited them if they surrendered, and proposing a conference of all the surviving officers. All his friend's captains agreed to the proposal except one, who said that their only hope was to win the trust of the Great King: anyone who said otherwise was talking nonsense. He was quickly chased away by the other captains. Then, in Xenophon's account:

> They went to the various contingents, and where the general was alive they invited the general; where he was missing they invited the second-in-command; and where the captain was safe they invited him. When they had all assembled there were about a hundred of them and by now it was nearly midnight.
>
> (XENOPHON, *Anabasis*, 3.1)

Then the oldest of his friend's captains asked Xenophon to repeat what he had said before.

So Xenophon made another stirring speech and persuaded them to elect new generals in place of those they had lost, and to call a meeting of the whole army at daybreak.

At this meeting Xenophon, who had been elected one of the generals and had put on his best suit of armour for the occasion, made yet another stirring speech. He ended with the following proposals. They should: burn all the wagons carrying their supplies; burn all their tents; burn all unnecessary baggage; all vote to support the officers in maintaining discipline; march in a hollow square, with the pack animals and non-combatants in the centre. These proposals were carried by a show of hands.

The first day's march

The first day's march was a disaster. Xenophon commanded the rearguard and describes his experiences thus:

> They had gone only a short distance when Mithradates [one of Cyrus' former friends] appeared with about 200 horsemen and about 400 archers and slingers. These were very quick and agile. Mithradates rode up as if he were a friend, but when his men had got close his horsemen and

foot soldiers suddenly began to shoot arrows or hurl sling-stones at the Greeks and wounded them.

(XENOPHON, *Anabasis*, 3.3)

Fig. 13. Persian soldier: depicted on wine bowl dated mid-fifth century.

Xenophon explains that the Greek rearguard could not fight back. Their archers had a shorter range than the Persian archers; besides, they had to take cover behind the infantry because they had no protection against the arrows and sling-stones (they wore no armour). The Greek javelin men, too, could not throw far enough to reach the enemy's slingers. So Xenophon decided that the only thing to do was to charge. This did no good either. Without cavalry the Greeks could not catch up even with the Persian infantry, while the Persian cavalry kept shooting as they rode away. So more Greeks were wounded. All that day the Greeks managed to march only eight miles. Just before evening they reached some villages and settled down for the night.

Improvisations

Morale was low, and Xenophon was blamed for risking the rearguard by charging away from the main body of the army without doing any harm to the enemy. He accepted the blame, but, looking, as always, on the bright side of things, he remarked that it would have been a great deal worse if the enemy had attacked in greater force. As it was the Greeks had learnt a valuable lesson at comparatively small cost. Thereupon he set about organising a troop of fifty horsemen, mounting them on captured cavalry horses which the Greeks had been using as pack-animals. He also went among the ranks looking for slingers and found 200 heavy-armed infantrymen who came from the island of Rhodes. Every boy born in Rhodes was trained to be a crack slinger, so Xenophon persuaded these Rhodians to put aside their heavy armour for the time and serve as slingers. The generals also organised a small shock force to be ready to charge without hesitation, as there would be a support force ready to back them up.

Revenge

The next day they rested. The day after they marched again, and Mithradates came with 1,000 horsemen and 4,000 archers and slingers. He had boasted to Tissaphernes, Xenophon says, that with these he would have no difficulty in rounding up the Greeks.

Mithradates caught up with the Greeks just after they had crossed a ravine. The Persians began to cross after them.

> Soon the Persians caught them up and the sling-stones and arrows were just beginning to reach the Greeks. On a trumpet signal the Greek shock troops charged and the horsemen charged and the enemy fled back to the ravine, losing many infantry killed and up to eighteen horsemen captured in the ravine. The Greeks, without being given orders to do so, mutilated the bodies of the dead Persians to frighten the enemy by the horrid sight.
>
> (XENOPHON, *Anabasis*, 3.4)

Progress

After that the Persians left the Greeks alone for several days. The Greeks continued to march up the left bank of the Tigris. They were now in what had once been the heartland of the Assyrian Empire and they passed the ruins of the once great cities of Nineveh and Calah. They were impressed by the magnificence of the walls, which were still standing, and by the remains of a ziggurat (Xenophon calls it a 'stone pyramid') nearby, but they knew nothing of the greatness of Assyria.

Soon after they had passed the deserted cities they encountered Tissaphernes again. He had, in addition to his own forces, the army which Artexerxes' half brother had brought up too late for the battle of Kounaxa. His army now included also the Asian troops who had set out with Cyrus, and he was accompanied by the King's son-in-law who was on his way to his province of Eastern Armenia. All these troops made up a huge army and they harassed the Greeks from a distance without doing them great harm. The Rhodian slingers found they could hurl their bolts further than the Persian slingers could hurl their much heavier stones, and even further than the Persian archers could shoot their arrows. The Cretan bowmen also learned to take a high elevation when shooting so that their arrows had a greater range and could not fail to fall on the massed ranks of Tissaphernes' troops. As they marched the Greeks experimented with different tactics to find out how best to march through narrow defiles without losing the cohesion of their ranks. Where possible the heavy-armed infantry flanked the baggage train and the non-combatants, but in a defile or crossing a bridge they learnt to fall back in well-disciplined units so as not to get jumbled up with the baggage and non-combatants. In the hilly country the heavy-armed infantry, the terror of the Persians on open ground, were an embarrassment, and the light-armed troops came into their own. The Greeks frequently found themselves having to march through narrow passes while hostile natives hurled rocks down on them from above. On such occasions the light-armed troops could be sent scrambling up the hillsides to take the natives in the rear and drive them off the hilltops, thus allowing the rest of the 10,000 to march unhindered through the pass below.

A crossroads

After many marches they came in sight of the mountains of Kurdistan. From prisoners they learnt that they were at a junction of four roads. Two of these would take them back into the heart of Persia, a third led towards Ionia, but to follow this road they would have to cross the Tigris in the face of Tissaphernes' army, which was not practicable. So the generals decided there was nothing for it but to take the fourth road which led into the high and rocky mountains. These were inhabited by the Kardoukhoi (the ancestors of the modern Kurds). They were very tough fighters and their country was so rocky and mountainous that they were virtually unconquerable. What the Greeks did not know was that the Persians had an agreement with them which gave them their independence (and subsidies) in return for not molesting traffic on the Persians' military roads, and supplying troops for the Persian army when needed. What the Greeks were told was that the Great King had once sent an army of 120,000 soldiers to punish them – presumably when they had violated the agreement – and not one soldier had come back. This last information the Greeks got from their prisoners.

Into the mountains

The Greeks hoped that, since both they and the Kardoukhoi appeared to be enemies of the Great King, the Kardoukhoi might be friendly towards them; but it was not so. Instead they attacked them with ferocity, rolling rocks down the mountainside as well as shooting at them with arrows and sling-stones. They were very agile and carried no arms or armour except their bows and slings. Their bows were nearly five feet long, and their arrows more than three feet long and these could go straight through a shield and breastplate. When the Greeks came across spent Kardoukhoi arrows, they fitted them with thongs and used them as javelins.

They soon discovered that the Kardoukhoi and their mountains were a formidable obstacle. The generals and captains decided that they must abandon all but the strongest pack animals, and all the prisoners they had recently taken. They gave orders accordingly. When the march began the generals stationed themselves in a narrow defile and took away anything that any of the troops had retained against orders. The only objections they encountered were when a soldier had smuggled in a boy or attractive woman he had taken a fancy to. (This is one of the rare occasions when Xenophon mentions the women who accompanied the Ten Thousand. All Greek mercenary soldiers took women with them when they went campaigning and the Ten Thousand were no exception. One modern scholar has commented that if the endurance of the Ten Thousand was remarkable, even more remarkable was that of their women.)

The river crossing

After seven days the Greeks found a comfortable bivouac in some well-provisioned villages in the hills overlooking a river. Since crossing this river would take them out of Kurdistan and into Armenia, they thought that the worst was over. They had suffered more casualties from the Kardoukhoi than they had suffered in all their fighting with the Persian army.

Disappointment, however, awaited them. At daybreak they saw that on the further bank there were Persian cavalry and infantry waiting to attack them as they crossed. To make matters more difficult the Kardoukhoi had followed them and were massing in their rear. The first time they tried to cross they found the river too deep and the river bed covered with large slippery rocks. So they camped for the night.

That night Xenophon had another of his dreams. This time he dreamed that he was in chains and the chains suddenly and spontaneously fell off. He told his dream to the Spartan general who had taken command of the vanguard (and presumably acted as commander-in-chief, though Xenophon never says so) and they both felt sure that the dream meant that things would turn out well. So Xenophon went off to have his breakfast – a time when any of the soldiers were at liberty to come up and speak to him. While he was breakfasting two young soldiers ran up with good news. They had been collecting firewood and had seen, on the other side of the river, an old man and a woman and some girls. These had been putting what looked like bags of clothes in a cave. They decided it was safe to cross because it was too rocky on the far side for the enemy cavalry to get near the river. So, keeping only their daggers with them, they stripped off their clothes to swim across. But when they went into the water they found that they could wade across without even wetting their private parts. So they had stolen the clothes and recrossed the river.

Knowing now that there was a shallow ford, the Greek generals made a plan to get most of the army across it, while Xenophon and his rearguard made a feint attack by the main ford where the Persians were waiting for them. This was about half a mile upstream. The plan worked and they drove off both the Persians on the far side of the river and the Kardoukhoi who charged down on them from the rear.

Marching in the snow

After crossing the river the Greeks marched for six days across flat
country or gentle hills. On their way they came across a large village
with plentiful provisions, a palace for the Governor and some fortified
houses. They were now in Western Armenia and Tiribazos, the
Governor, rode up with a squadron of horsemen to make a truce. He
would let the Greeks march through his district unharmed if they
promised not to burn the houses. The Greeks agreed. They marched
on and came to another palace surrounded by more well-supplied
villages.

> While they were bivouacked in this place so much snow fell
> during the night that it was decided next morning that the
> troops with their officers should move into the villages and
> bivouac there, since there was no sign of the enemy and the
> extent of the snow seemed a protection in itself. Here they
> found provisions of all sorts: beef, corn, vintage wines (very
> fragrant), raisins and peas, beans and lentils. Some,
> however, of the troops who had wandered from the camp
> claimed that they had seen an army and that many fires had
> appeared during the night. So the generals decided it was
> unsafe to have the troops bivouac in scattered villages and
> that they should be reassembled to spend the night in the
> open. During the night there was a heavy snowfall which
> covered both the piled arms and armour and the men
> themselves as they lay on the ground, while the feet of the
> pack animals were frozen together. None of the men
> wanted to get up, since they were warmed by the snow as
> long as it actually covered them. Xenophon [he always
> writes of himself in the third person], with a great effort,
> got up and started splitting logs, stripped to the waist.
> Seeing him, another man got up and, taking the log from
> him, split it himself. Thereupon they all got up and made
> themselves fires and rubbed themselves with ointments
> which they had found in the village and which they used as
> they would olive oil. The ointments were of many sorts:
> pigs' fat, sesame, bitter almonds and turpentine. There was
> also a balm made from all of these.
>
> (XENOPHON, *Anabasis*, 4.4)

It was now early winter and the snow got worse and worse as they
marched onwards. They lost many baggage animals, many of the
captives and about thirty of the troops. Many others suffered from

frostbite, snow-blindness or hypothermia. These had to be forcibly prevented from lying down to die.

An underground village

Eventually they came to a village in which all the houses were underground. The entrances were just like the mouth of a well. Humans climbed down by ladder, but there were tunnels for the animals. Goats, sheep, cattle and chickens were all kept in the houses and fed on winter fodder. There were plenty of provisions and much strong drink, so the Greeks feasted and caroused for seven days. The barley-wine was kept in huge bowls. The natives sucked it through straws or reeds which were left floating on top of the liquor; the Greeks, however, ignored the straws. Whenever anyone, in a spirit of comradeliness, wanted to offer a drink to a friend, he took him to a bowl and made him stoop and gulp it 'just like an ox', as Xenophon puts it.

On the eighth day they set off again, taking the village headman and his son with them – the headman as a guide and his son as a hostage. The headman showed them how to wrap bags round the hooves of the horses and other pack animals to prevent them from sinking into the snow. However he did not guide them to any other villages. The Spartan general got angry about this and hit him. That night he slipped away leaving his son behind. The Greek soldier who was guarding the son had fallen in love with him. Eventually he took him home to Greece and kept him as a loyal comrade for life.

The sea at last

After losing their guide the Greeks marched for nine days through the mountains, covering about fifteen miles a day. They had to fight to capture the pass that led down to the plain, but did so with few casualties because they had sent troops ahead by night to capture the high ground above the pass. Xenophon called this 'stealing the mountain' and teased the Spartan general, saying that he should be particularly good at it since Spartans were from boyhood taught to steal – and only punished when caught – as part of their military training. The Spartan retorted that according to his information all Athenians were expert thieves since they elected their magistrates from among those who were cleverest at stealing the public funds without getting caught. So now was the time for Xenophon to show himself a true Athenian.

Between them they successfully 'stole' the mountain and marched through the pass and down into the plain, where they found well-supplied villages. This, however, was only a brief respite as there was more mountainous country ahead with mountaineers who defended their homes with fanatical courage. When the Greeks finally overwhelmed their defences, all the adults committed suicide hurling first their children, then themselves over precipices onto the rocks below.

After marching for three weeks, with a halt of three days to stock up with provisions, the Greeks came to yet another mountain. As soon as they reached the top the men in front began to shout. Xenophon was in his usual place with the rearguard.

> When Xenophon and the rearguard heard the shouting they thought that a new enemy must be attacking the van of the army...the shouting, however, grew louder and nearer, and others, coming up towards those who were shouting, kept breaking into a run to join them. The shouting, as more and more men joined in, became still louder. Xenophon thought it must be something serious, so he leaped onto his horse, and, taking the cavalry and their commander with him, he went to help. Then they soon heard what the men were shouting. It was 'Thalassa! Thalassa!' 'The sea! The sea!'
>
> (XENOPHON, *Anabasis*, 4.7)

So the Ten Thousand knew that safety was almost within their grasp. What they saw was the Black Sea, where there were Greek colonies, and where they could expect to find ships to take them back to Greece.

Epilogue
Sequels

The Ten Thousand

The last part of the journey to the Black Sea was made easy because of an unexpected piece of luck. After descending from the mountain from which they had seen the sea, they came to a river. The banks of the river were covered with dense thickets of small trees and the further bank was lined with natives armed with spears and wicker shields. These were jabbering away to one another and throwing stones into the river without harming anyone since they all fell short. At this point one of the light-armed troops came up to Xenophon to say that he seemed to understand the language they were speaking, and this must be the country where he had been born and from which he had been taken to Athens as a slave (and presumably freed to serve as a soldier in the Athenian forces). He asked permission to speak to the natives. 'By all means,' said Xenophon, 'and ask them who they are and why they are hostile to us.' He did so and they replied that they were Makrones and they were hostile because the Greeks were trying to invade their country. The generals then told him to say that they had no intention of harming anyone but merely wanted a passage to the sea. So to everyone's satisfaction they exchanged a Greek spear for a Makronian spear (the Makrones' method of pledging their word) and the Makrones sold them food to the best of their ability and guided them through their country. They had one more fight against the Kolkhians and an adventure with some intoxicating honey, after which they arrived to a warm welcome at the Greek city of Trapezos.

There they made to Zeus and Herakles the sacrifices they had promised if they escaped from the Persians. They also celebrated their safety with a festival of games – wrestling, running (long and short distance), boxing and horse racing.

Soon afterwards they held a review and counted the troops. They found that 8,600 had survived the march.

So far so good. Afterwards they had a long period of quarrels with the Greek cities of the Black Sea, with Spartan officials who had been sent from Sparta to take charge of the Greek cities, and among themselves. They took to plundering the neighbouring tribes, and went campaigning for a Thracian king who cheated them of their pay.

Eventually the Spartans declared war on Persia, and most of the remaining mercenaries joined the Spartan army.

Xenophon

Xenophon stayed with the mercenaries until he became rich through a plundering raid against a Persian noble. Later he became friends with the Spartan king who was commanding the Spartan army in its war against Persia. In this war the Athenians took the Persian side, so they banished Xenophon. He went to live near Sparta, on land which the Spartans gave him. There, in gratitude for coming safely through so many dangers, he built a temple to Artemis, and held a yearly festival in her honour.

Tissaphernes

After marching away from the Greek mercenaries on the upper Tigris, Tissaphernes went to govern the provinces which had been governed by Cyrus. When the Spartans declared war on Persia he was constantly defeated. Parysatis had managed to get into her power and torture to death all the Persian officers who had helped to kill Cyrus on the battlefield. Now that Tissaphernes was discredited she encouraged Artaxerxes to have him treacherously seized (in his bath) and executed.

Artaxerxes

After treatment from Ktesias he recovered from the wound which Cyrus had given him and reigned for 46 years. His mother Parysatis succeeded eventually in her long-standing ambition to poison his wife Statira (or so we are told by Plutarch who got it from Ktesias). She then encouraged him to marry his own daughter Atossa with whom he had fallen in love.

As a ruler he fought – through his generals – an unsuccessful war against the Spartans, until he discovered that he could achieve much more by subsidising the Greek states to fight one another. In this way he obliged the Spartans to make a peace treaty which returned the Ionian cities to Persian rule. Also through his generals he attempted to recover Egypt which had revolted from the Empire before he became king; but this expedition was a failure. Late in his reign he commanded in person a campaign against a people called the Kadousioi who lived in the north-east of the Empire and had been in revolt for thirty years. This was a failure also, and he had to be rescued by the resource of that Tiribazos whom the Greeks encountered in Western Armenia. However Artaxerxes had shown by his leadership in danger and hardship that his character had not been sapped by the luxury and ceremony of court life.

The conclusion of Artaxerxes' reign was beset by palace intrigues – or so we are told by Plutarch, who is supposed to have got his information from Dinon. When Cyrus' camp at Kounaxa had been overrun by the Persians they had found Cyrus' women among all the other luxuries that a Persian prince took with him when on campaign. One of them, a Greek from Miletos, escaped minus her clothes from the midst of the Persians to the Greek troops who were guarding the mercenaries' baggage. (Presumably she afterwards shared the hardships of the Ten Thousand.) Another woman, who did not escape, was Cyrus' favourite mistress, a Greek from Phokaia, celebrated for her wit and wisdom as well as for her beauty, and nicknamed Aspasia – the name of Pericles' mistress (who had been famous for her intellectual accomplishments as well as for her beauty). After her capture at Kounaxa, Cyrus' Aspasia became a favourite of Artaxerxes. When Artaxerxes in his old age came to designate a successor, he chose his eldest son Darius. According to Persian custom Darius, on being declared heir, was entitled to ask a favour. He asked for Aspasia. Reluctantly Artaxerxes said that she might choose between them. To Artaxerxes' annoyance she chose Darius, so, soon afterwards, he got his own back by appointing her to be a priestess of the goddess Anaitis, whose worship he, unlike his predecessors, promoted. This office constrained Aspasia to chastity and the appointment was regarded by Darius as a provocation. Tiribazos (who was in and out of disgrace throughout the reign) had been likewise provoked when Artaxerxes promised to him in marriage, firstly his daughter Amestris and then his daughter Atossa, but ended by marrying both himself. So the two entered into a conspiracy which was betrayed. Tiribazos was killed strenuously defending himself: Darius tried to escape but was captured and executed. To complete Plutarch's story, Artaxerxes' second son, Okhos, had seduced Atossa and with her encouragement he got rid of his remaining two brothers and, on his father's death, became king as Artaxerxes III.

Greece

The mainland Greeks spent the next sixty years fighting brutal wars against one another. Sparta, Thebes and Athens were each top dog in turn. North of Greece the half-Greek kingdom of Macedon was becoming steadily stronger, and in 335 BC King Philip of Macedon utterly defeated the armies of Thebes and Athens. In 334 BC his son Alexander the Great led a Macedonian and Greek army into the Persian Empire and conquered it. He burnt Persepolis in revenge for the burning of Athens 150 years earlier.

Persia

The Ten Thousand had begun the age of the mercenary soldier. The Greek states in their wars against each other took to hiring their armies. These had to be paid if they were not to desert to the enemy. So rich Persia kept Greece weak by paying the city-states to enable them to go on fighting one another. Persian governors hired mercenaries to help them to revolt against the Great King and the Great King hired them to put down the revolt. The mercenary armies were commanded by capable soldiers who were also resourceful politicians and knew when to change sides to the greatest advantage to themselves. When Artaxerxes III set out to reconquer Egypt, once unsuccessfully and once successfully, Greek mercenaries were fighting on both sides.

Artaxerxes III had begun his reign by murdering all those of his relatives who had a claim to the throne. In his lifetime he recovered much of the power and authority of the monarchy over its widespread and unruly dominions.

Five years after the reconquest of Egypt he was poisoned by one of his army commanders who was a eunuch. Not content with half measures, the eunuch then murdered all Artaxerxes' sons and grandsons, leaving only a distant cousin to take the throne as Darius III. Darius murdered the eunuch and became king just in time to be defeated three times by Alexander the Great and then murdered by some of his own nobles.

For the next two hundred years the Persian Empire was ruled by the descendants of Alexander's generals. From the time of Christ all the western half was ruled by the Roman emperors and the eastern half by Parthian (Iranian) kings.

Suggestions for Further Study

The religion and customs of the Persians

Herodotus (1.131-40) describes Persian religious practices and social customs. The description is most significant in showing which Persian attitudes and practices seemed surprising to a Greek. J.M. Cook in *The Persian Empire* has a chapter on Persian religion which has much more information than was available to Herodotus. In *Greece and the Hellenistic World* (ed. Boardman, Griffin and Murray) there are chapters on religion and on life and society in Classical Greece.

What are the points of contrast between Greek and Persian religion?

The reliability of Herodotus

Greece and the Hellenistic World has a chapter on the Greek historians, which discusses Herodotus and suggests further reading. *The Cambridge Ancient History* Volume IV offers opinions which suggest that historians of Persia place less faith in him than do historians of Greece. Hignett in *Xerxes' Invasion of Greece* gives another view of the reliability of Herodotus.

What are the main arguments for and against trusting Herodotus?

East versus West

Rudyard Kipling, who knew India very well and wrote many stories about encounters between Englishmen and Indians – both men and women – wrote also a *Ballad of East and West* in which occur the well-known lines:

> East is East and West is West, and never the twain shall meet
> Till Earth and Sky stand presently at God's great Judgement Seat.

H.G. Wells in *A Short History of the World* (ch. 19) wrote:

The theme of history from the ninth century BC onward for six centuries is the story of how...Aryan peoples grew to power and enterprise and how at last they subjugated the whole Ancient World, Semitic, Aegean and Egyptian alike. In form the Aryan peoples were altogether victorious; but the struggle of Aryan, Semitic, and Egyptian ideas and methods was continued long after the sceptre was in Aryan hands. It is indeed a struggle that goes on through all the rest of history and still continues to this day. [Wells was writing in 1922.]

Man, State and Deity (Methuen, 1974) is a collection of essays by Victor Ehrenberg. The first essay is 'East and West in Antiquity'. It discusses the interaction of Western and Eastern ideas from pre-historic times to the reign of the Emperor Justinian (AD 527-65). Ehrenberg writes:

It is...the contrast of two different spiritual aspects, two ways of the working of the human mind. If we are prepared to see it in its most sweeping (and therefore inaccurate) generalisation, we can speak of the god-centred East and the man-centred West.
It goes without saying that those relations and conflicts could be political, economic, social, religious or of any other sphere of man's life and mind...history has been shaped by the relations and decisions between East and West to such an extent that behind the various historical forces lies a certain unity, though not uniformity...There can be little doubt that the foundations laid in those centuries are, even if unconsciously, the foundations of all succeeding times.

Try investigating, with the help of one or two general histories, such as Wells' *A Short History of the World* or Fisher's *History of Europe*, some of the traces of the interaction of East and West.

Is Christianity an eastern or a western religion?

Was the Byzantine Empire eastern or western?

Were the Arab Caliphates in Spain in the Middle Ages eastern or western?

Byzantine Art – was it eastern or western? If it was eastern, when, how and why did western ideas set it on the path to become the art of the Italian Renaissance?

These are all open questions to which there cannot be simple answers. Nevertheless try to sketch out some possible answers.

Oriental monarchies

It is believed by some scholars that the concept 'Oriental Monarchy' is misleading, if not meaningless, and should be abandoned. For most of us the words conjure up the picture of a monarch who exercises power without restraint, lives in self-indulgent luxury and magnificence and possesses a harem. The harem implies eunuchs (who are at the centre of power but can only exercise it through others), illegitimate, as well as legitimate, sons (which tends to provoke bloody succession struggles) and the probability of excessive feminine influence, usually capricious and baneful, on state policy.

Racine, whose *Bajazet* is referred to on page 65, wrote his tragedies at the court of Louis XIV of France. Louis XIV, after the early difficulties of his reign, exercised almost unlimited power. He ruled France through ministers who were humbly born and therefore could only exercise power and influence as his creatures and at his pleasure. He lived at Versailles in extravagant splendour, campaigned in style and comfort, and, although a pious Christian, had a great number of mistresses and several illegitimate sons. These illegitimate sons intrigued to hold power after his death as regents for his great grandson Louis XV. In his last years he married one of his mistresses and under her influence he undertook the persecution of the Huguenots: a policy which is regarded by historians as disastrous for its effects on French prosperity.

Apart from the fact that he had no harem (in name at least) and therefore no eunuchs, do you think the rule of Louis XIV can have been significantly different from that of the Achaemenid monarchs as described in J.M. Cook's *The Persian Empire* (see especially ch. 13, 'King and Court') and Plutarch's biography of Artaxerxes II? If it was different, would you attribute this to different traditions of kingship in East and West? Or to the influence of Christianity? Or to limitations imposed on the ruler of one European state competing with others (England, Spain, Austria, The Netherlands) by contrast with the ruler of a vast empire with no comparable rivals? Or to the existence in Europe of a class of literate intellectuals and a tradition of controversial writing that might be muzzled but could not be suppressed?

And if there is no significant difference, to what would you attribute the not infrequent assumption among historians that there have been, since the dawn of history, many 'Oriental Monarchies' quite unlike anything ever to be found in the West?

The character and truthfulness of Xenophon

George Cawkwell in his introduction to the Penguin translation of Xenophon's *Persian Expedition*, expresses scepticism about the reliability of Xenophon's narrative as an untouched-up account of what actually happened, and as a guide to the military and political strength of the Persian Empire. Much of what Cawkwell says is incontrovertible and a valuable warning against a naïve acceptance of Xenophon's narrative as plain truth. Yet the Persian Empire did collapse very rapidly less than seventy years later under the impact of Alexander. Similarly, unless all the accounts of Persian affairs between, say, the death of Cambyses and the final victory of Alexander are false, treachery and cruelty must have been a regular feature of life for the Persian aristocracy. Cawkwell's attempt, therefore, to whitewash the treatment by Tissaphernes of Klearkhos and the Greeks may not seem totally convincing. As to the remarkable fact that the account of the expedition of the Ten Thousand by Diodorus the Sicilian never once mentions the name of Xenophon, that – considering the nature of Diodorus' working methods – may not conclusively prove that Xenophon's role was really quite insignificant.

The arguments are recondite and complex, and one would be rash to challenge the conclusions of a historian of Cawkwell's penetrating and erudite scholarship. They make fascinating reading and can be compared with a slightly less sceptical account of Xenophon and his truthfulness which is to be found in Stephen Usher's introduction to *Xenophon: the Persian Expedition* (BCP, 1978). J.M. Cook in *The Persian Empire* seems to accept the essential correctness of Xenophon's account of the deeds and intentions of the Persians towards the Ten Thousand. Xenophon and his *Persian Expedition* are also discussed briefly by Oswyn Murray in the chapter on Greek historians in *Greece and the Hellenistic World*.

All four scholars write attractively, so a comparison of their expressed, or implied, views could be pleasurable as well as intellectually rewarding. Which do you find most persuasive? Why?

Alexander's conquest

Taking the widest possible view it seems difficult, though just possible, to argue (and it has been so argued) that humanity would have been better served if Xerxes had been successful in conquering Greece. On the other hand the effect of Alexander's victories was to destroy a relatively stable empire which conferred peace and prosperity on a remarkably large area of the world, and allowed its subjects a great amount of personal and civic liberty. In its place the successors to Alexander's short rule gave Asia Minor the experience of constant warfare as they disputed large fragments of his empire between themselves, and continued outbreaks of campaigning even after they had reached a more or less stable division, into three great monarchies, of what had been Alexander's Empire. It is true that Alexander's conquests took Greek settlers and Greek culture into widespread communities throughout the area of former Persian rule, but the Persian monarchy had already shown itself able to absorb much of Greek, as well as Babylonian and Egyptian culture.

Consider the possible arguments for regarding both Xerxes' failure and Alexander's success as misfortunes for humanity.

Achaemenid art

Compare the Palace and Temple Art and Architecture of Egypt, Greece, Assyria and Achaemenid Persia. What special character-istics, do you think, are shown by the relics of the Achaemenids? (A visit to the British Museum should be helpful.)

Suggestions for Further Reading

Original sources in translation

Herodotus, *The Histories*, translated by A. de Selincourt, 2nd edition with an introduction by A.R. Burn (Penguin, 1972).

Xenophon, *The Persian Expedition*, translated by R. Warner with an introduction and notes by G. Cawkwell (Penguin, 1972).

Plutarch, *Lives of Themistocles, Aristides, and Cimon* in *The Rise and Fall of Athens*, translated by I. Scott-Kilvert (Penguin, 1960).

Plutarch, *Life of Artaxerxes*. This has not so far been translated in the Penguin series and is only available in the Loeb series, vol. 11, trans. B. Perrin (Heinemann, 1926).

Modern historical works

Burn, A.R., *Persia and the Greeks* (2nd edn. Duckworth, 1985). A full and attractive narrative beginning with the Assyrian Empire and ending with the Battle of Plataea. The introduction discusses Herodotus and Ktesias and the epilogue takes in the Peace of Kallias. The second edition has a postscript by D.M. Lewis updating some details with reference to the Persepolis tablets.

Cook, J.M., *The Persian Empire* (Dent, 1983). A very lucid and readable account. It pieces together a coherent story of the middle and later years of the Achaemenid monarchy by drawing on what relevant Greek sources there are. This results in a view of the Empire which is now under challenge. Good maps and photographs.

Cook, J.M., *The Greeks in Ionia and the East* (Thames and Hudson, 1962). This has all the virtues of *The Persian Empire* and is solidly based on the considerable and ever increasing archaeological evidence. It portrays the culture of the Ionian cities, before and during their subjection to the Persians, during the domination of Athens (a bleak period) and in their fourth century revival. Especially good on the art and architecture, it turns the reader's attention from campaigns and conquests to the source of the true interest of these centuries. There are many admirable illustrations: both photographs and line drawings.

Hammond, N.G.L., *A History of Greece to 322 B.C.* (OUP, 1959). One of Hammond's main interests is military history. Chapters 3 and 4 of Book 3 of his *History* give a lucid and carefully considered account of the campaigns of the Persians against the Greeks and of the individual battles.

Frye, R.N., *The Heritage of Persia* (Weidenfeld, 1962). This has 50 pages on the Achaemenid period. Gives the arguments for both sides on controversial matters. Good descriptive matter on religion, court, bureaucracy, economic and military organisation.

Briant, P., *Alexandre le Grand*, (3rd edn, Presses Universitaires de France, 1987). Good incidental material on the Persian Empire in the account of the resistance to Alexander (according to Briant the conquest was no pushover). Brief (125 small pages) and to the point, but it has to be read in French as, so far, there is no translation.

Boardman, J., Griffin, J., Murray, O. (eds), *Greece and the Hellenistic World* (Oxford History of the Classical World, OUP, 1988). Probably the most useful general survey of the Greek background to the clash between Greece and Persia, both for its text and for its splendid illustrations. Ch. 8, on the Greek historians, is particularly relevant.

Hignett, C., *Xerxes' Invasion of Greece* (OUP, 1963). 74 pages of 'Prolegomena' discuss the sources and their critics. Hignett is highly critical of Herodotus' accounts of Thermopylae and Salamis, which are discussed at length.

Lewis, D.M., *Sparta and Persia* (Brill, Leiden, 1977). Six lectures on various topics, e.g. Satraps and their journeys (material from the Persepolis tablets), relations between Sparta and Persia, economics of the Empire, Persian queens. He is prepared to take Ktesias seriously on some matters.

Hornblower, S., *The Greek World 479-323 BC* (Methuen, 1983). Ch. 1 is on the effects on Greece of Xerxes' invasion and ch. 6 on Persian relations with Asia Minor. Ch. 2 has two pages (pp. 18-19) on medism. Hornblower's writing is too dense with information to make an easy read, but in these sections readers will find some stimulating challenges to traditional and simplistic views of the relations between Greeks and Persians.

Usher, S., *The Historians of Greece and Rome* (H. Hamilton, 1969, repr. BCP 1985). Chapters on Herodotus and Xenophon which make some interesting points.

Gould, J., *Herodotus* (Historians on Historians series, Weidenfield, 1989). Priority reading. Gould's approach is that of the field anthropologist who seeks to understand a culture by identifying with it. He has the effect of making much previous scholarly comment seem obtuse, egocentric and irrelevant.

For reference

Hornblower, S., *Mausolus* (OUP, 1982). This biography of the ruler in whose honour the Mausoleum of Halikarnassos was built contains a wealth of detail on the Persians' organisation of the western part of their Empire. Too lengthy and dense for a relaxed read, it is a useful quarry for significant detail.

Cambridge Ancient History vol. 4 (2nd rev. edn, CUP, 1988). This volume assembles the up-to-date scholarship on both sides of the Greco-Persian confrontation and must be for some time to come the most valuable of resources for anyone wondering how much he can believe of what he finds in the pages of Herodotus.

Cambridge History of Iran vol. 2 (CUP, 1985). The only narrative chapter is a condensed version of A.R. Burn (op. cit.). Other chapters are on e.g. pre-Achaemenid Elam, Media and Egypt, the Behistun relief, religion, coinage, the Persepolis tablets.

Ghirshman, R., *Persia from the Origins to Alexander the Great* (Arts of Mankind series, Thames and Hudson, 1964). There are two chapters (40 pages) on Achaemenid art. Sumptuous photographs.

Articles and chapters

(These may be hard to come by, but they should be available from the Ancient History Bureau of the Joint Association of Classical Teachers (31-34 Gordon Square, London WC1H OPY) for members.

Kuhrt, A., 'The Achaemenid Empire: a Babylonian Perspective' in *Proceedings of the Cambridge Philological Society* 214 (ns 34) 1988. Puts in a nutshell (12 pages) the problems in writing Achaemenid history.

Sancisi-Weerdenburg, H., 'Decadence in the empire or decadence in the sources? From source to synthesis: Ctesias' in *Achaemenid History I: Sources structures and synthesis* ed. Sancisi-Weerdenburg, H. (Leiden, 1987).

Stevenson, R.B., 'Lies and inventions in Deinon's Persica' in *Achaemenid History II: the Greek sources* ed. Sancisi-Weerdenburg,

H. and Kuhrt, A. (Leiden, 1987).

Kuhrt, A., 'Earth and Water' in *Achaemenid History III: Method and Theory: Proceedings of the London 1985 Achaemenid History Workshop* ed. Kuhrt, A. and Sancisi-Weerdenburg, H. (Leiden, 1988). A close look at the significance of the Persians' demand for earth and water from states on the fringe of their empire.

Sancisi-Weerdenburg, H., 'Exit Atossa: images of women in Greek historiography on Persia' in Cameron, A. and Kuhrt, A. (eds) *Images of Women in Antiquity* (Croom Helm, 1983). Radical and fascinating on Persian queens as they appear in Greek writings. It dismisses Herodotus' Artaynte episode as the attachment of a folk-tale (which incorporates various anthropological motifs) to some rebellion within the Persian royal family.

Fiction

Renault, M., *The Persian Boy* (Penguin, 1974). An unforgettable *tour de force* of the imagination. There are even scholars who admire it.

Vidal, G., *Creation* (pbk. Grafton Books, 1982). The fictitious autobiography of a Persian nobleman, born half-Greek half-Mede, grandson to Zoroaster, boyhood friend of Xerxes, later royal emissary to India, China and Greece. It views Greco-Persian conflicts as if through the wrong end of a telescope, seeing them as insignificant incidents, grossly overrated by the boastful and untrustworthy Greeks. The characters are lively and entertaining but cut out of cardboard by comparison with those of Mary Renault.